Cordon Bleu

Cooking
with Eggs

Cordon Bleu

Cooking
with Eggs

Macdonald and Jane's
London

Published by
Macdonald and Jane's Publishers Ltd
Paulton House
8 Shepherdess Walk
London N1

This impression 1977

Designed by Melvin Kyte
Printed by Waterlow (Dunstable) Ltd

These recipes have been adapted from the Cordon Bleu Cookery Course
published by Purnell in association with the London Cordon Bleu
Cookery School
Principal : Rosemary Hume ; Co-Principal : Muriel Downes
Quantities given are for 4 servings.
Spoon measures are level unless otherwise stated.

Contents

Introduction

Cordon Bleu cooks would get nowhere without eggs, for they go into every form of cooking — breakfast, lunch, tea and dinner, main course, starter, drinks and dessert, cakes and pastries, pasta and puddings. In fact, cooking with eggs is really just cooking.

But, as a start, we have collected together in this book some of the ways eggs are used as the main ingredient in a dish. We have left out the uses of eggs in cakes, sauces and other mixtures, and concentrated on the delights of omelets and soufflés and the multitude of dishes based on simple boiled, poached or scrambled eggs.

This way we hope to get you thinking about eggs in their own right. For one of the techniques of Cordon Bleu cooking, based on the French concept of home economics, is the maximum use of basic ingredients. Eggs are comparatively cheap, they keep well, and they have a very high nutritional value. So French housewives take advantage of this and use them in every way possible to vary and enrich the diet of their families. We know the standard English home has eggs for breakfast — the French don't do that, but they have them at every other conceivable time, in every imaginable guise. How else could they eat so well in a country where home budgets are often severely limited and food prices are high ?

This book can be only an introduction to this most versatile of foods. But we hope that even experienced cooks will find something new to add to their repertoires. With a dozen eggs in the refrigerator you need never be at a loss to feed the family, or to entertain casual droppers in as handsomely as though you had known they were coming.

Rosemary Hume
Muriel Downes

7

Basic egg cookery

We all know that eggs are good for us, but it probably brings it home that much more convincingly if we stop to think that an egg actually becomes a chicken. In concentrated form it contains everything that goes to make up body tissues — high proportions of protein and fat, calcium, iron, the most vital amino acids and all the major vitamins except C. Eggs have the added advantage of being easily assimilable, which is why they play such an important part in invalid diets.

When we talk about eggs for eating, we normally mean hen's eggs. The eggs of other birds are, of course, equally edible, but they are either too small to be worth the bother or, as with the eggs of bigger birds, the flavour is very strong. If you do like duck, or goose, eggs, and can get them, they are excellent for cake making and good in many other dishes as well. But do remember to alter the amount of other ingredients in proportion to the size of the egg. An average hen's egg weighs 2 oz, whereas a duck's weighs 3 oz and a goose's 8-10 oz.

Eggs should be eaten as fresh as possible ; you can tell a new-laid one (up to one week old if kept in a cool place) by breaking the shell ; if fresh, the white will cling to the yolk. To test an egg without first having to break it, plunge it into cold salted water (use kitchen salt) ; if very fresh the egg will sink at once ; the staler it is the higher it will float (bad ones floating on top). As eggshells are porous, a certain amount of liquid evaporates every day, resulting in a lighter egg ; fresh ones when shaken should feel heavy and well filled.

Boiled eggs
(Œufs à la coque)
There is quite an art in boiling an egg — though many people still say that if they can't cook, they can at least boil an egg ! However, many things can go wrong : the white may be runny, the yolk too set, or worst of all, the shell may crack in the water so that most of the white escapes.

Points given here should help you avoid these pitfalls. One answer is, of course, an egg-timer — but don't, like a young bride we knew, put the timer in the pan with the egg.

1 Make sure that the shells are perfectly clean. If not, wash or wipe with a damp cloth.
2 Choose an enamel pan for boiling eggs because they will blacken an aluminium one. If an aluminium pan has to be used, a little vinegar added to the water will prevent this. Vinegar will also prevent the white seeping away if the eggs crack, which is especially likely with preserved eggs.
3 Never take the eggs straight from a refrigerator or cold larder. Leave eggs at room temperature for a while, so that they are warm, before putting them into boiling salted water.
4 Boil eggs steadily but gently for $3\frac{1}{2}$-4 minutes according to taste. Allow $3\frac{1}{2}$ minutes for a lightly boiled egg, and 4 minutes for one that is well set. Take the time from when the water reboils after adding eggs to pan.

It is generally reckoned that

the slower the white cooks, the more digestible the egg. In this case, put the eggs into a pan of cold water and bring them slowly to the boil. Allow a further 30 seconds of gentle simmering, when the eggs will be lightly cooked.

Coddled eggs

Put eggs into a pan of boiling water, cover, take off heat and leave for 5 minutes. Eggs cooked in this way will have a soft, creamy white and are ideal for children and invalids.

To make sure egg is cooked if you have no timer, an old-fashioned trick is to lift the egg from the water and count eight. If the shell becomes dry, the egg is coddled.

Soft-boiled eggs
(Œufs mollets)

Many dishes, both hot and cold, can be made from soft-boiled eggs. For these dishes the eggs are cooked a little differently.

1 Put eggs into a pan of boiling water and allow 5 minutes from time water comes back to the boil. Remember, though, that a small egg will take less time to cook through.
2 Take them out at once and put into cold water for 7-8 minutes. Then peel carefully.
3 The eggs may be used straight away. If you want them hot, they may be left (unpeeled) in hand-hot water for 5 minutes. If you want them cold, peel and leave in cold water for several hours until required.

As these eggs are delicate to peel, first crack the shells gently all over with the back of a spoon. This will soften the shell and make it easier to take off without breaking the egg. Once cracked all over, peel off a band

across the middle of the egg. You will then find that the shell at each end of the egg can be pulled off.

Hard-boiled eggs
(Œufs durs)

Always put eggs in boiling water and allow 10-12 minutes steady boiling, but no longer, because over-boiling discolours the yolks and toughens the whites. Plunge them at once into cold water, which will make the eggs easier to peel, however fresh they are. Peel as for soft-boiled eggs.

To stuff hard-boiled eggs : cut them lengthways after peeling and scoop out the yolks with the handle¨ of a teaspoon. Put the whites at once into a bowl of cold water to keep them tender and white.

When required, carefully lift out whites and lay them, cut side downwards, on a clean cloth to drain. If serving cold stuffed eggs, it is easier if the halved whites are arranged in place on the serving dish before filling with the prepared mixture. This will give a better and neater result. Stick them to the surface of the dish with a little of the filling.

Once the halved whites are filled, an alternative way of dishing them up is to put them together to reshape the egg. Dish up as for the halved whites. If serving boiled eggs under a sauce, especially if it has to be glazed or browned, the eggs should be slightly softer. Before coating them with a sauce, dry eggs well on absorbent paper or a cloth, otherwise the sauce will slide off. Make sure, too, that the sauce, particularly mayonnaise, is of a good coating consistency.

Buttered or scrambled eggs
(Œufs brouillés)

These should be soft, creamy and melting and this depends largely on the amount of butter added. Don't add too much milk as this is inclined to give a curdled, watery effect.

To 4 eggs allow 1 good oz of butter and 3 tablespoons of single cream or creamy milk. Beat eggs well with a fork, adding milk, salt, pepper and half the butter in small pieces.

Melt remaining butter in a pan, pour in the egg mixture and cook over moderate heat, stirring and scraping the mixture from the bottom of the pan with a spoon, preferably metal, to get thick, creamy flakes. Take care not to overcook eggs. Turn them on to buttered toast while they are still creamy.

Here's an alternative way for those who do not like too rich a mixture. Put the butter and milk into the pan first (here a little more milk may be used) and, when hot, break in the eggs and allow the white to set lightly before stirring. Then season and stir mixture to break up eggs and continue cooking until the scrambled eggs are thick.

Fried eggs
(Œufs frits)
You can fry these eggs in either shallow or deep fat.

Shallow frying : make sure that the fat (not less than $\frac{1}{4}$ inch in the pan) is not too hot. If it is, it will toughen the whites. Break the eggs, one at a time, into a cup and gently slide them into the pan. Cook on moderate heat, basting with the fat, until both white and yolk are set. To speed the process, the pan may be put under a hot grill for a few seconds.

Deep fat frying : half fill a small deep pan with fat. Heat until 400°F (oil to 360-375°F), then gently tip in the eggs and cook for 2-3 minutes until golden-brown. Drain the eggs very carefully. For the best results, do not fry more than two at a time.

Poached eggs
(Œufs pochés)
New-laid eggs are best for poaching, otherwise the white will detach itself from the yolk. Poach eggs in a saucepan or deep frying pan filled with boiling water — add about 1 tablespoon vinegar to 1 quart of water. Do not add salt as this tends to toughen the white.

Keep heat low and water gently simmering, then break eggs into pan and poach for about $3\frac{1}{2}$-$4\frac{1}{2}$ minutes until firm. Lift out with a draining spoon or fish slice and drain thoroughly before dishing up.

Egg poachers are available but the above method is satisfactory as the eggs do not stick (which sometimes happens in a poacher) and are less obviously 'moulded' in shape.

French poached eggs are well-shaped, plump and round. The above directions apply except that the eggs should be poached, one at a time, in deep water which has been stirred gently immediately beforehand. The action of the water brings the white up, over and round the yolk. The egg is then lifted out and put into warm water unless it is served immediately.

Poached eggs, like soft-boiled eggs, can be kept several hours in cold water before use. To reheat the eggs, lift into a bowl of hand-hot water and leave for 4-5 minutes before taking them out and draining.

13

For cold poached eggs the whites must be really firm, the yolks should just give under gentle pressure.

For hot poached eggs to be served under a sauce, especially if it has to be glazed or browned, the eggs should be slightly softer. Dry eggs well on absorbent paper or cloth before dishing and coating with a sauce, otherwise the sauce will slide off.

Baked eggs
(Shirred eggs — œufs en cocotte or sur-le-plat)
These are delicious and may be cooked and served in individual buttered cocottes, ramekins or soufflé dishes or in a shallow flameproof dish.

In their simplest form they have a little melted butter and cream, or creamy milk, poured over the yolks after the eggs have been broken into a buttered and seasoned dish. They are then baked in the oven at 350-375°F or Mark 4-5 for 6-8 minutes.

For a more substantial dish and an excellent way of using up leftovers, just break eggs on to a savoury mixture.

If eggs are cooked in shallow flameproof dishes they can be started on top of the stove and finished in the oven, when the white has begun to set, for 4-5 minutes further cooking.

Watchpoint Do not overcook as eggs will continue cooking after the dish has been removed from the oven.

Omelets

An omelet is one of the most useful egg dishes, ideal for a quick lunch or supper. It is quite easy to make and delicious whether plain or stuffed. As with all things, though, there is a secret that some cooks miss their whole lives through, per-

petually turning out rubbery messes in place of the delicious savoury they had hoped for.

The secret lies in using really fresh eggs and a good omelet pan. The pan must be kept for omelets only and never washed. If you fry other foods in it, it will have to be washed, which will cause your omelets to stick.

A true omelet pan is made either of thick aluminium or cast iron. The characteristic of the omelet pan is its curved edge, which makes the omelet easier to turn out and gives it a better shape.

A 3-4 egg omelet is probably as big as you will be able to handle without breaking it, and for this a 7-8 inch diameter pan is best. Any larger and the omelet will be thin and dry; smaller, and it will not cook through properly. 3-4 eggs are usually enough for two people.

When buying an omelet pan, wash it well, dry it and cover the bottom with salad oil. Leave for at least 12 hours, then heat the oil to frying point; remove the pan from the heat, pour off the oil and wipe the pan thoroughly with absorbent paper.

After this, don't wash the pan again; after each use, wipe it round with a damp cloth, or paper towel, dipped in salt. This will season the pan and prevent your omelets from sticking.

There are two types of omelet, the plain, or French, omelet and the fluffy, or soufflé, one. French omelets are generally savoury either plain or stuffed; occasionally they are filled with jam, but this is rare. Often the savoury omelet is served as a light lunch or supper dish, sometimes as a first course; the more substantial ones, such as Spanish omelet, are ample for a main course. The soufflé omelet is usually served with a sweet sauce or filling, as a dessert.

A good savoury omelet should be what the French call 'baveuse' — slightly runny. There are people, however, who do not like eggs unless they are cooked really firm. In this case it is best to use the soufflé omelet method normally reserved for desserts (see pages 122-123), because a French omelet cooked until firm becomes tough.

Plain omelet

4 **eggs**
1½ **tablespoons cold water**
salt
black pepper (ground from mill)
1 **oz butter**

7-8 inch diameter omelet pan

Method
Break eggs into a basin and beat well with a fork. When well mixed, add water and seasoning (this should be done just before cooking). Heat pan on medium heat. Put in butter in two pieces and, when frothing, pour in egg mixture at once. Leave for 10-15 seconds before stirring round slowly with the flat of a fork. Do this once or twice round pan, stop and leave for another 5-6 seconds.

Lift up edge of omelet to let any remaining raw egg run on to hot pan. Now tilt pan away from you and fold over omelet to far side. Change your grip on pan so that the handle runs up the palm of your hand. Take the hot dish or plate, in your other hand, tilt it slightly and tip omelet on to it. Serve at once.

Stirring eggs with flat of fork

Starting to turn omelet over

Folding over, with the pan tilted

Tipping omelet on to a plate

Herb omelet

(Fines herbes omelet)

This is a delicious omelet, especially in summer when herbs are fresh.

Method

Make as for a plain 4-egg omelet and add 1 rounded tablespoon of mixed chopped herbs (parsley, thyme, marjoram or tarragon, and chives) before pouring mixture into pan. Snip chives finely with scissors rather than chopping them. The mixture should be quite green with the herbs.

Cheese omelet

Make as for a plain 4-egg omelet and scatter 2-3 tablespoons grated cheese thickly over omelet whilst in pan, just before folding it over. A mature Cheddar or Gruyère is best.

STUFFED OMELETS

Make these in the same way as a plain omelet and spread the stuffing mixture quickly over omelet before folding it over. A little of the mixture, such as tomato or mushroom, can be reserved to spoon over centre of omelet when turned out.

The following recipes are for 4-egg stuffed omelets.

Note : for basic method for making an omelet see previous page.

Tomato omelet

2-3 tomatoes (peeled and sliced)
$\frac{1}{4}$ oz butter
salt and pepper
mint (chopped) — to garnish

Method

Sauté tomatoes in butter in a pan for 1-2 minutes. Season well and add a good sprinkling of mint before spooning into omelet. Don't overcook tomatoes.

Mushroom omelet

3 oz mushrooms (sliced or quartered)
$\frac{1}{4}$ oz butter
2 rounded teaspoons flour
3-4 tablespoons stock, or water
salt and pepper
squeeze of lemon juice

Method

Slice or quarter mushrooms, sauté 2-3 minutes in butter in a pan. Stir in flour, add liquid and seasoning, stir until boiling. Then add lemon juice. The consistency should be creamy. Make a plain omelet, pour in mushroom mixture before folding omelet over.

Potato omelet

1-2 medium-size potatoes (diced)
$\frac{1}{4}$ oz butter
few leaves of rosemary (optional)

Method

This can be made with cooked or raw potato. Dice finely and brown in butter ; add rosemary while frying. Make a plain omelet and spoon in potato before folding over.

Bacon and croûton omelet

2-3 tablespoons bread (finely diced) — for croûtons
¼ oz butter
3-4 rashers of bacon (diced)

Method
Fry diced bread in butter in a pan until golden-brown. Take out and fry the diced bacon until crisp. Mix together with croûtons. Make a plain omelet and spoon in bacon mixture before folding over.

Bacon and potato omelet
(Bonne femme)

2 medium-size potatoes
1 small onion
2-3 rashers of bacon
¼ oz butter
salt and pepper

Method
Dice potatoes, slice onion finely ; cut bacon across into strips. Melt butter in a pan, add potatoes, onion and bacon. Season, cover pan and cook slowly for 7-8 minutes, or until potatoes and onion are tender and slightly brown. Stir occasionally.
Make plain omelet, spoon in mixture before folding over.

Omelet Arnold Bennett

4 eggs (separated)
4 tablespoons smoked haddock (cooked and flaked)
2 oz butter
¼ pint cream
salt and pepper
3 tablespoons grated Parmesan cheese

This is an elegant dish which was created for the writer, Arnold Bennett, by the Savoy Grill in London. It is one of the best omelets.

Method
Toss the haddock with 1 oz butter and 2 tablespoons cream in a pan over a quick heat, for about 2-3 minutes, allow to cool.
Beat the egg yolks with 1 tablespoon cream and season. Whip the egg whites lightly, fold into the yolks with the haddock, add half the cheese.
Melt the rest of the butter in the pan and cook omelet. Do not fold, but slide omelet on to a hot dish, sprinkle on rest of cheese and pour the cream over it. Brown quickly under a hot grill and serve at once.

Spanish omelet 1

5 eggs (well beaten)
5 tablespoons olive oil
3 oz raw lean ham, or gammon
rasher (chopped)
1 Spanish onion (thinly sliced)
1 clove of garlic (crushed with
½ teaspoon salt) — optional
6 oz (about 2-3) potatoes (thinly
sliced, or coarsely grated)
salt and pepper

*This Spanish omelet, with ham and
potatoes, is cut in wedges for
serving with peperoni*

A true Spanish omelet is made on a base of potatoes and onion, then cooked in olive oil and well flavoured with garlic. Another version includes cooked mixed vegetables and is good for making use of leftovers. The consistency of both these omelets is firm, but not too solid. It is cut into wedges, like a cake, for serving.

Method
Heat the oil in a frying pan, add the ham, or rasher, cook for a few minutes, then add the

onion and a little of the crushed garlic to taste, if wished. Fry gently until the onion is half cooked, then add the potato. Season well ; cook until soft.

Drain off any superfluous oil and add beaten eggs to pan. Stir to mix, then cook until the underneath of omelet is brown. When the mixture is barely set, slide the pan under the grill to brown the top surface. When well browned, turn out omelet on to a flat dish.

Cut into wedges and serve with peperoni (see below).

Peperoni

2 green and 2 red peppers
  (halved, cored, seeds removed
  and thinly sliced)
1 oz butter
1 medium-size onion (sliced)
1 clove of garlic (crushed with
  $\frac{1}{2}$ teaspoon salt)

Method

Prepare the peppers and blanch if wished. Melt the butter in a small pan, add the onion and crushed garlic and cook slowly until soft but not coloured, add the peppers and seasoning and cook until just tender.

Spanish omelet 2

5 eggs
4 tablespoons olive oil
2 cloves of garlic (whole)
1$\frac{1}{2}$ cups cooked mixed vegetables
  — eg. small carrots (diced),
  potatoes (sliced), peas, sweet red
  peppers (sliced)
$\frac{1}{2}$ cup tomatoes (skinned, seeds
  removed and sliced)
salt and pepper

Method

Heat a large frying pan, put in the oil and garlic. Fry the garlic gently, then remove it. Put in the mixed vegetables and tomatoes and shake over heat until thoroughly hot.

Mix the eggs well with a fork in a basin, season and pour into the pan. Stir the mixture, then leave on gentle heat until the eggs are set.

Loosen omelet with a fish slice, then brown the surface under the grill. Slide omelet on to a flat serving dish.

Omelet Barante

6-8 eggs
1 small freshly cooked lobster
(poached in court bouillon —
see page 136)
6 oz firm white mushrooms
2-3 oz butter
salt and pepper
2 ½ fl oz port
1 small carton (2 ½ fl oz) double
cream
½ pint light mornay sauce (made
with milk flavoured as for
béchamel sauce) — see page 136
3-4 tablespoons freshly grated
Parmesan cheese

This delicious omelet was dedicated to the Baron de Barante, a famous 19th century gourmet.

Method

Crack claws and remove shell from lobster. Cut the tail meat into scallops. Wipe the mushrooms, trim stalks level with the caps and slice evenly. Sauté these in half the butter for 4-5 minutes, then season lightly. Add port, cover and boil the liquid hard to reduce to half quantity, draw aside and pour in the cream. Add the lobster meat, cover and simmer for 4-5 minutes, then draw aside.

Prepare the mornay sauce. Break the eggs into a bowl and beat to a light froth, add 2 tablespoons water and season. Make the omelet (see page 17), using the rest of the butter. While it is still soft and creamy in the middle, spoon in the lobster mixture, then roll up and turn on to an ovenproof dish for serving. Coat at once with the sauce, sprinkle well with the freshly grated cheese and brown under the grill. Use the head shell and tail meat of lobster to garnish the dish — or use small lobsters, if available.

Spooning lobster and mushroom filling into the omelet Barante before rolling it up to finish

Turning out the finished omelet. Omelet Barante is shown (right) with a garnish of small lobsters

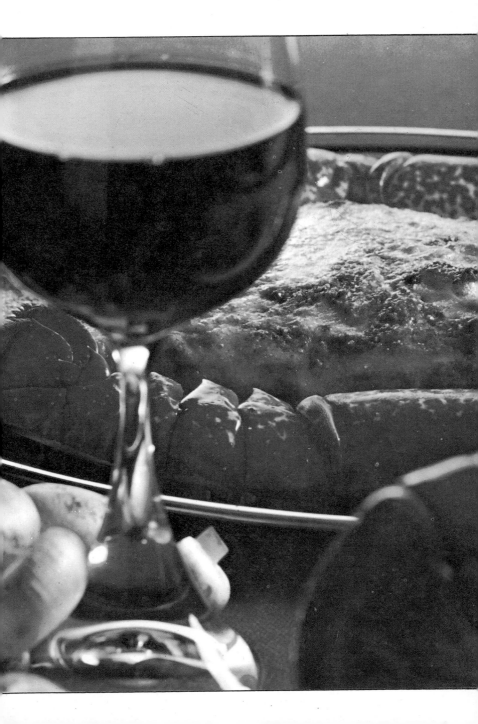

Parsee omelet

4 eggs
2 egg yolks
1 medium-size onion (finely chopped)
3 oz butter
2 tablespoons chopped coriander leaves
1 green chilli (seeded and finely chopped)
1 clove of garlic (crushed)
pinch of ground ginger
salt
2 tablespoons infusion of tamarind

To infuse tamarind add a piece of tamarind about the size of an egg to $\frac{1}{2}$ teacup of boiling water; leave for 10 minutes, then squeeze through muslin.

Method
Fry the onions to a pale gold in the butter in a large omelet pan. Beat the eggs and yolks together slightly and stir in the coriander, chilli, garlic, ginger and a large pinch of salt, and mix in tamarind infusion. Pour the egg mixture over the onions in the pan, stir mixture and tip pan until the mixture is set, but do not overcook it. Slide omelet from the pan on to a hot flat dish and serve at once, either plain, or with a salad.

For an easily made but unusual omelet, try this spicy Indian recipe

Soufflés and roulades

Light and fluffy on top, rich and gooey in the centre — that's how a soufflé should be. It's not so difficult to achieve, though, if you follow the rules. The most important of these is 'don't keep it waiting' — once your soufflé is cooked it will not wait while late guests arrive, or while the family collects itself — you must serve it at once or you are lost. Similarly with a roulade — a soufflé mixture baked on a flat sheet with a raised edge and then rolled up like a swiss roll.

So, sad as it may seem, this delicious savoury is not a good choice for that special dinner party unless you know your guests are people who are always punctual — keep it for everyday occasions when the family are there before you start to cook !

Rules for making savoury soufflés

1 Choose the right size soufflé dish or case for the quantity of mixture being made. Dishes are generally numbered 1-3, and the equivalent diameters are :

No. 1 — 7-inch diameter top
No. 2 — 6-inch diameter top
No. 3 — 5 $\frac{1}{2}$-inch diameter top
Before baking, the dish should be two-thirds to three-quarters full of the mixture.

2 Prepare the dish by rubbing the inside lightly with butter, and

Having rubbed inside of dish with butter, for savoury soufflé dust with browned crumbs; wrap grease-proof paper band round with a 2-inch fold at base and 3-inch overlap to keep it upright

Top : Tying paper band round to stand 2-3 inches above rim of the dish
Above : A little of the egg white is first folded in to soften the mixture

dust with browned crumbs (this makes it easier to clean).

3 To allow the soufflé to rise 2-3 inches above the dish when baked, cut a band of doubled greaseproof paper, about 6-7 inches wide and long enough to overlap about 3 inches round the side of the dish. Make a 2-inch fold along one long side.

Butter the strip above this fold, and wrap the paper round the outside of the dish, the fold at the base and turned inwards. This will keep the paper upright and firm. The greased section of the paper should stand above dish by some 3 inches.

Tie paper securely with string and set the dish on a baking sheet before filling. The string should be untied and the paper peeled off just before serving.

4 It is the whipped egg whites that make a soufflé rise, so it is important to whip them well. Ideally you should use a copper bowl and a light wire whisk. Whisking by hand in a bowl of this shape (see photograph below left) gives more bulk to whites. If you do not have a copper bowl, use a wire whisk with a china or earthenware bowl, never a rotary whisk or mixer.

5 When adding egg whites to the mixture, stir in a small quantity with a metal spoon before the main bulk is added. This softens the mixture so that when the remaining whites are added the whole remains light and fluffy.

6 Pre-heat the oven to 375°F or Mark 5. Arrange the shelves so that the soufflé can be placed in the centre with no shelf above it. This will give it plenty of room to rise. To avoid any unnecessary opening of the oven door, try not to cook anything else when a soufflé is inside.

7 When cooked, the top should be evenly brown and firm to the touch, the consistency lightly firm, with the centre soft and creamy. Serve it straight from the oven — better keep the family waiting than the soufflé.

To make roulades

Make the roulade mixture as if for a soufflé, but bake it either in a swiss roll tin lined with greaseproof paper, or in a paper case. To make the paper case, follow the pictures below and overleaf. When the roulade is cooked, turn it out of its case on to a sheet of greaseproof paper, peel off the paper on which it was cooked, spread with the appropriate filling, and roll it up.

Use thick greaseproof paper or non-stick (siliconised) cooking paper. Fold a 1½ -inch border on each side, crease into place

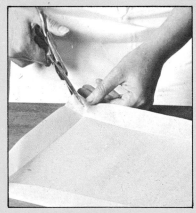

Cut a slit at each corner and fold one cut piece over the other to mitre the corners of the paper case

27

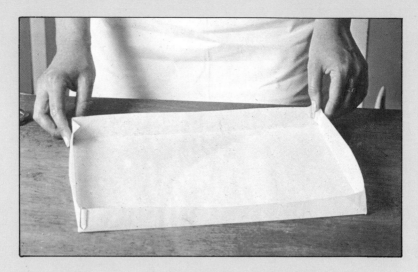

Secure corners with paper clips and slide case on to a baking sheet. Lightly brush paper case with oil or melted butter before use

Cheese soufflé

4 rounded tablespoons grated
  cheese
1½ oz butter
1 rounded tablespoon plain flour
salt
cayenne pepper
¾ cup of milk
1 teaspoon ready-made mustard
4 egg yolks
5 egg whites
1 tablespoon browned crumbs
  (raspings)

*7-inch diameter top (size No. 1)
soufflé dish*

Ideally the cheese used should be a mixture of grated Parmesan and Gruyère. Otherwise use a dry Cheddar.

For browned crumbs (also known as raspings) bake several crusts of bread in a slow oven until golden-brown. Crush or grind them in a mincer. Sift crumbs through a wire bowl strainer to make them uniformly fine, then store in a dry, screw-top jar.

Method

First prepare soufflé dish. Set oven at 375°F or Mark 5.

Choose a medium to large saucepan. Make a roux by melting the butter, removing pan from heat and stirring in the flour. Season well, blend in milk. Put pan back on heat, stir until boiling then draw aside. Add mustard and beat in 3 rounded tablespoons cheese and egg yolks one at a time.

Watchpoint The basic sauce must be well flavoured with cheese and well seasoned to compensate for the amount of whites added.

When well mixed, whip egg whites to a firm snow, stir 2 tablespoons of the whites into the sauce, using a metal spoon. Then stir in the remainder in two parts, lifting the sauce well over the whites from the bottom of the pan. Turn the bowl round while mixing ; do not overmix.

Turn lightly into prepared soufflé dish. Quickly dust top with crumbs and rest of cheese mixed together. Bake for 25-30 minutes in pre-set oven, until evenly brown and firm to the touch. Serve immediately.

Italian soufflé

1 oz butter
1 rounded dessertspoon plain flour
salt and pepper
¼ pint milk
6 tablespoons grated cheese
3 egg yolks
4 egg whites
1 tablespoon browned crumbs
— see page 29

For filling
1 oz spaghetti
salt and pepper
4 tablespoons strong tomato sauce
(see page 140), or 1 dessertspoon
tomato purée
½ oz butter

6-inch diameter top (size No. 2)
soufflé dish

Italian soufflé — made with alternate layers of spaghetti in a tomato sauce before dusting with browned crumbs and baking in oven

Flaked cooked fish or shredded cooked ham, etc. can be used in place of the spaghetti.

Method

Prepare the soufflé dish. Simmer the spaghetti in a large pan of boiling salted water until tender (about 12 minutes). Drain and rinse with a cup of hot water. Drain again and return to the pan.

Shake over heat with $\frac{1}{2}$ oz butter for 2 minutes, then season well and add the tomato sauce or purée. Stir with a fork until the spaghetti is well coated with tomato. Set aside.

Set the oven at 375°F or Mark 5. Make the soufflé mixture as for cheese soufflé (see page 29), using all the cheese.

When mixture is complete, turn enough into dish to cover the base, add half the spaghetti and cover this with half of the remaining soufflé mixture. Add rest of spaghetti and top with rest of soufflé. Dust with browned crumbs and bake for 25-30 minutes in pre-set oven, until evenly brown and firm to the touch.

Mushroom soufflé

8 oz flat mushrooms, or mushroom stalks (finely chopped)
1 oz butter
1 tablespoon freshly chopped mixed herbs (parsley, mint, chives)
salt and pepper
4 egg yolks
5 egg whites
1 tablespoon grated cheese
1 tablespoon browned crumbs
(see page 29)

For béchamel sauce
$1\frac{1}{2}$ oz butter
1 rounded tablespoon plain flour
$\frac{1}{2}$ pint milk (infused with 1 slice onion, $\frac{1}{2}$ bayleaf, 6 peppercorns, 1 blade of mace, a few pieces of carrot)

7-inch diameter top (size No. 1) soufflé dish

Method

Prepare the soufflé dish. Set oven at 375°F or Mark 5.

Wash mushrooms but do not peel, chop them finely. Cook in 1 oz butter in a fairly large pan for 4-5 minutes. Increase heat, if necessary, to drive off any excess liquid. Add herbs and seasoning.

Prepare béchamel sauce (see page 136) and stir into the mushroom mixture.

Beat the egg yolks into the béchamel and mushroom sauce mixture, one at a time. Whip whites to a firm snow, cut and stir 1 tablespoon of these into the mixture, using a metal spoon. Then stir in remainder.

Turn into the prepared dish. Sprinkle top with cheese and browned crumbs mixed together and bake for 25-30 minutes in pre-set oven.

Spinach soufflé

1½ lb spinach, or 1 large packet of frozen spinach purée
½ oz butter
salt and pepper
pinch of ground mace, or grated nutmeg
3 egg yolks
4 egg whites
1 tablespoon grated cheese
1 tablespoon browned crumbs (see page 29)

For sauce
1 oz butter
1 rounded tablespoon plain flour
salt and pepper
¼ pint milk

7-inch diameter top (size No. 1) soufflé dish

This is a basic recipe for a vegetable soufflé. Other vegetable purées — cauliflower, carrot, celeriac — can be used instead of spinach. Allow 8-10 rounded tablespoons of purée to the above quantity of sauce. For a bland vegetable, such as cauliflower, 1 tablespoon of a sharp grated cheese (Parmesan, dry Cheddar) in the mixture is an improvement.

Method

Prepare the soufflé dish. Set oven at 375°F or Mark 5.

Trim and wash spinach, boil in salted water for 8 minutes, drain and press well. Pass through a sieve, turn back into pan and stir over moderate heat to drive off excess moisture. Add the butter, season and set pan of spinach aside.

If using frozen spinach, put into a large pan on a gentle heat until completely thawed. Then increase heat to drive off excess moisture, add butter, seasoning and set aside.

To prepare sauce : make a roux by melting the butter, removing pan from heat, stirring in flour, then season and blend in milk. Add this to the spinach with the mace or nutmeg and additional seasoning to taste.

Beat in the egg yolks one at a time. Whip the whites to a firm snow, then cut and stir 1 tablespoon into the mixture, using a metal spoon. Stir in remainder of whites and turn into the prepared dish. Sprinkle top with cheese and browned crumbs mixed together. Bake for 25-30 minutes in pre-set oven until well risen and firm to the touch.

Fish soufflé

1 lb whiting (filleted)
3 egg yolks
salt and pepper
pinch of ground mace
1 tablespoon double cream
4 egg whites
1 tablespoon browned crumbs
  (see page 29)

For béchamel sauce
½ oz butter
1 tablespoon plain flour
¼ pint flavoured milk (see
  mushroom soufflé, page 31)

*7-inch diameter top (size No. 1)
soufflé dish*

Method
Prepare soufflé dish and set oven at 375°F or Mark 5.

Fillet the whiting or ask the fishmonger to do it, remove skin and bone, and shred flesh finely.

Prepare the béchamel sauce (see page 136).

Watchpoint Avoid overcooking béchamel; it should just come to boiling point — no more — then allow it to cool.

Place fish in a mortar or bowl, add cold béchamel sauce a little at a time and pound mixture well. Beat in egg yolks one at a time. Then rub mixture through a wire sieve or work in a blender until smooth and velvety. Season, add mace and stir in cream.

Whisk the egg whites until stiff and then, using a metal spoon, stir 1 tablespoon into the mixture to soften it; then quickly and lightly stir in the rest. Turn at once into prepared soufflé dish and dust top with browned crumbs. Bake for 25-30 minutes in pre-set oven. Serve with crab or lobster sauce.

Crab or lobster sauce

1 small can (approximately 3 oz)
  crab, or lobster meat
1 oz butter
1 rounded tablespoon plain flour
1 teaspoon paprika pepper
¼ pint fish stock (made from
  bones and trimmings of
  whiting)
¼ pint milk
1 tablespoon sherry
1 tablespoon double cream
salt and pepper

Method
Drain crab or lobster meat, break it up carefully with a fork, removing any membranes, and keep on one side.

Melt butter in a pan, stir in flour and cook gently until honeycombed in appearance. Add paprika and cook for a few seconds (take care not to scorch it).

Draw pan aside and blend in the stock, return pan to heat and stir until sauce begins to thicken; then add milk and bring to boil. Cook for 2-3 minutes.

Heat crab or lobster meat in sherry in a pan and add to sauce with the cream. Adjust seasoning.

Spinach roulade

1 lb spinach
½ oz butter
salt and pepper
4 eggs (separated)
Parmesan cheese (grated)

For filling
6 oz mushrooms (thinly sliced)
½ oz butter
1 rounded dessertspoon plain flour
salt and pepper
¼ pint milk
nutmeg (grated)
2-3 tablespoons cream (optional)

*Swiss roll tin (12 inches by 8 inches),
or paper case*

Method
Line tin with buttered greaseproof paper, or make a paper
case. Set oven at 400°F or
Mark 6.
Cook spinach in boiling salted
water for about 8 minutes, drain
well, press and sieve.
Stir in butter, seasoning and
the yolks of the eggs, one at a
time. Whip the whites to a firm
snow and fold into the mixture.
Turn the mixture on to tin or
case, spread out to about ½ inch
thick and dust with cheese. Bake
in pre set oven for about 10 min
utes until well risen and firm.
Meanwhile prepare the filling :
slice unpeeled mushrooms thinly,
sauté in butter, remove from heat
and add the flour with seasoning
to taste. Pour on the milk and
bring to the boil, simmer to a
creamy consistency, draw pan
off heat. Stir in a little grated
nutmeg and cream, if wished.
Remove cooked roulade from
oven, turn out on to a sheet of
greaseproof paper, quickly peel
off the paper on which it was
cooked, spread with the mushroom filling and roll up.

Smoked haddock roulade

8 oz (2 cups) smoked haddock
(cooked and flaked)
4 eggs
3 rounded tablespoons grated
cheese

For filling
béchamel sauce (made with 1½ oz
butter, 2½ tablespoons plain flour,
¾ pint flavoured,or plain, milk)
salt and pepper
1 dessertspoon anchovy essence
3 eggs (hard-boiled and finely
chopped)

*Swiss roll tin (12 inches by 8 inches),
or paper case*

Tunny fish, canned or fresh
salmon or crab meat may be
used in this dish.

Method
Line tin with buttered grease
proof paper, or prepare paper
case. Set oven at 400°F or
Mark 6.
Prepare the filling : make
béchamel sauce (see page 136),
season and add anchovy
essence. The sauce should be
creamy and thick enough just
to drop from the spoon.
Take 3 tablespoons of sauce
and add to the cooked fish.
Add the chopped eggs to the
remaining sauce ; cover and set
aside but keep warm.
Separate eggs and beat yolks
into the fish with one-third of
the cheese. Whip whites to a
firm snow and cut and fold into
fish mixture, with a metal spoon.
Put on to the tin and spread
evenly. Bake on top shelf of
pre-set oven for 10-15 minutes
or until well risen and firm to the
touch.

Have ready a large sheet of greaseproof paper, sprinkled with the remaining cheese. Quickly turn the roulade on to this, strip off the paper it was cooked on and spread roulade with the filling. Trim off sides, then tilt paper and roll up mixture in the same way as for a swiss roll (see photograph 3). Put on to a hot serving dish and sprinkle with additional cheese, if wished.

1 Beating egg yolks and cheese into the fish and sauce mixture
2 Spreading uncooked fish mixture evenly over roulade case
3 Rolling up haddock roulade after spreading on its creamy filling (see finished dish on page 36)

Pancakes and waffles

For another egg treat, turn to pancakes, water thin and lacy round the edges. A festival food for years in Europe, where it is the central food of many Shrove Tuesday carnivals, the simple pancake is often forgotten at other times of the year. But with sweet or savoury fillings, full of nourishing eggs, milk and butter, what could be better to fill a hungry family ?

Or try the favourite American waffle, a slightly more substantial version of the pancake, using bicarbonate of soda and baking powder. For this you need a special waffle iron, which cooks the batter on both sides at once, and moulds a pattern into the surface.

Pancakes don't have to be made and served straight away. Not only the batter, but the pancakes themselves, can be made several hours or even the day before they are wanted, so long as they contain a good proportion of eggs and butter. Kept in an airtight container and reheated properly they taste as if freshly cooked.

For your pan, choose a small one, with a base about 6 inches in diameter, made of cast iron or aluminium. To make tossing easier, choose one with shallow sides. Like an omelet pan, the pancake pan should not be washed out (in fact, you could use the same pan for both if it is a small one). Just wipe the pan with a damp cloth or paper dipped in salt, and rub lightly with a few drops of oil.

Basic pancake batter

4 oz plain flour
pinch of salt
1 egg
1 egg yolk
½ pint milk
1 tablespoon melted butter, or
  salad oil

Method
Sift the flour with the salt into a bowl, make a well in the centre, add the egg and yolk and begin to add the milk slowly, stirring all the time. When half the milk has been added, stir in the melted butter

37

or oil and beat well until smooth.

Add the remaining milk and leave to stand for 30 minutes before using. The batter should have the consistency of thin cream — if too thick, add a little extra milk.

To cook the pancakes, you will need very little fat in the pan — wipe out pan before setting over moderate heat and when it is thoroughly hot put in just a few drops of oil. Take 1 tablespoon of the batter and tip this into the pan, immediately rolling it round clockwise to coat the bottom evenly. (This quantity will be enough for a 6-inch diameter pan.)

Cook until the underneath of the pancake is a good brown colour. Run a palette knife under the edges to loosen the pancake, then raise it slightly with the fingers and slip the knife underneath. Flip the pancake over and cook for about 10 seconds on the other side. If you feel brave, try tossing the pancakes instead !

When cooked, turn them onto a rack and stack them up, one on top of the other, until you have as many as you want (two per person is usually enough). If you are not going to use them immediately, cover the stack with a bowl, or wrap in a tea towel. If they are for use the following day, store in foil or a polythene bag with a sheet of greaseproof or waxed paper between each pancake.

To reheat pancakes melt about 1 oz butter, brush this on to a baking tray, then peel off the pancakes and lay them overlapping along the tray. Brush well with more melted butter to exclude the air and protect the pancakes during cooking.

Put the baking tray into the oven at 400°F or Mark 6 for 3-4 minutes. For pancakes with a stuffing, stuff them while cold and bake them with the stuffing in for 7-10 minutes.

If all the batter is not used, keep it covered and use within three days.

Chicken pancakes with curry

For pancake batter
3 oz plain flour
pinch of salt
1 egg
1 egg yolk
7½ fl oz milk
1 tablespoon melted butter, or
salad oil

For curry sauce
½ pint milk
bouquet garni
6 peppercorns
1 small onion
½ small carrot
small stick of celery
1 oz butter
1 rounded teaspoon curry
powder
½ oz plain flour
salt

For filling
½ lb chicken meat (cooked and
shredded)
1 egg (hard-boiled and chopped)

For finishing
2 tablespoons double cream
1 tablespoon grated Parmesan
cheese

Method
Prepare pancake batter (see method, page 37), leave for 30 minutes in a cool place.

To make curry sauce: scald milk in pan with bouquet garni and peppercorns, cover and leave to infuse for 5 minutes, then strain and rinse pan. Cut the vegetables into small dice, put in a saucepan with a good half of the butter and cook slowly until soft but not coloured ; then add the remaining butter and curry powder and cook for a further 2-3 minutes. Blend in the flour and add flavoured milk, add salt and stir until boiling. Simmer for about 10 minutes, then strain into a basin.

Mix the shredded chicken and chopped egg with about two-thirds of the sauce. Keep warm.

Set oven at 400°F or Mark 6. Fry pancakes and stack them on a warm dish. Put a tablespoon of filling in the centre of each pancake, fold them in four and arrange in a buttered oven-proof dish.

Add the cream to the remaining curry sauce and pour it over the pancakes. Sprinkle with the cheese and bake in the pre-set oven until brown and crisp (for 7-8 minutes).

Ham pancakes

½ pint pancake batter (see page 37)

For filling
½ lb flat mushrooms
2½ oz butter
1 shallot (finely chopped)
1 teaspoon plain flour

2½ fl oz stock, or single cream
salt and pepper
1 tablespoon chopped parsley and
thyme (mixed)
8 thin slices of ham
1 tablespoon grated Parmesan
cheese

Method

Prepare pancake batter, leave in a cool place for 30 minutes.

Wash the mushrooms quickly in salted water, drain and chop finely. Melt 1 ½ oz butter, add the shallot and cook until soft but not coloured, then add the mushrooms and continue cooking until all the moisture has evaporated. Blend in the flour and stock or cream; season and bring to the boil. Add the herbs.

Set oven at 400°F or Mark 6. Fry pancakes and place a slice of ham and a large tablespoon of mushroom filling on each one, fold two sides to the centre, then fold in half. Place in a buttered ovenproof dish, melt remaining butter and brush or pour over the pancakes.

Sprinkle with the cheese. Bake in pre-set oven for 7-10 minutes.

Left : selection of ingredients for making savoury ham pancakes
Below : place slice of ham on the cooked pancake, then a large tablespoon of filling in the middle. Fold two sides to the centre, then fold in half for final baking

Pancakes Beatrix

For batter
3 ½ oz plain flour
pinch of salt
2 eggs
2 tablespoons melted butter, or
  salad oil
¼-½ pint milk
1 oz Gouda cheese (finely grated)

For filling
2-3 smoked trout
béchamel sauce (made with 1 oz
  butter, 1 oz plain flour, ½ pint
  flavoured milk) — see page 136
salt and pepper
1 teaspoon horseradish cream —
  see page 137
1 tablespoon double cream

For finishing
3 tablespoons double cream
1 tablespoon grated Parmesan
  cheese

Method

Make the batter as in basic recipe (see page 37), adding the grated cheese when half the milk has been added. Leave to stand for 30 minutes in a cool place.

Remove the skin and bone from the trout and divide into neat fillets. Make béchamel sauce, season, then add the horseradish cream and tablespoon of double cream.

Set the oven at 375°F or Mark 5. Fry paper-thin pancakes, fill each one with the fillets and sauce, roll up like cigars and arrange in a buttered dish. Spoon over the extra cream, dust with Parmesan cheese and bake in the pre-set oven for about 10 minutes. Serve very hot.

Spinach pancakes

½ pint pancake batter (see page 37)

For filling
1 lb spinach
1½ oz butter (plus a little melted)
1 shallot (finely chopped)
2 teaspoons tomato purée
4 tomatoes (peeled and roughly chopped)
1 teaspoon paprika pepper
4 eggs (hard-boiled and sliced)
salt
black pepper (ground from mill)
1 tablespoon grated Parmesan cheese

Method
Prepare pancake batter, leave in a cool place for 30 minutes.

Cook spinach in plenty of boiling water, drain thoroughly and set aside.

Melt 1 oz butter, add shallot and cook slowly until soft but not coloured. Stir in tomato purée, tomatoes and paprika pepper and simmer for 2-3 minutes. Add slices of hard-boiled eggs and season.

Fry thin pancakes and spread with spinach, heated through in butter. Put 1 tablespoon of egg mixture on each one and roll up.

Place in a hot ovenproof dish, sprinkle with a little melted butter and grated cheese and brown lightly under the grill.

Stuffed cabbage pancakes

½ pint pancake batter (see page 37)

For filling
1 small, or ½ large, Dutch cabbage (weighing about 1½ lb)
1 onion (sliced)
1 oz butter
4 oz salt belly pork (cooked until tender and cut in strips), or unsmoked streaky bacon (cut in lardons and blanched)
4 tablespoons stock (see page 139)
salt and pepper

For mornay sauce
1 oz butter
1 rounded tablespoon plain flour
½ pint milk
2 oz grated cheese

Method
Prepare the batter and leave to stand in a cool place for 30 minutes. Fry pancakes as for basic recipe (see page 37) and set aside.

Trim the cabbage, cut in four, discarding stalk, and shred finely. Put onion in a heavy flameproof casserole or pan with the butter, cover and cook slowly until soft. Add the pork or bacon and cook until golden-brown. Stir in the cabbage and stock, season, cover with a buttered paper and lid and cook slowly on top of stove or in the oven at 350°F or Mark 4 until tender (about 40 minutes).

Prepare the mornay sauce (see page 138) reserving 1 tablespoon cheese.

Fill pancakes with cabbage mixture, fold in half and place in a buttered ovenproof dish. Coat with mornay sauce, sprinkle with the cheese and bake in pre-set oven at 400°F or Mark 6 until golden-brown (7-10 minutes).

Crêpes écossaises

$\frac{1}{2}$ pint pancake batter (see page 37)

For filling
1 lb smoked haddock fillet
$\frac{1}{2}$ pint milk
2 eggs (hard-boiled)
1 shallot (sliced)
$\frac{1}{2}$ blade of mace
2 oz butter
1$\frac{1}{2}$ oz plain flour
salt and pepper

To finish
1 oz butter (melted)
1 oz grated Parmesan cheese

Method

Prepare the batter and leave to stand in a cool place for 30 minutes. Fry pancakes as for basic recipe (see page 37) and wrap them in a clean dry teacloth until the filling is prepared. Cover the smoked haddock with water, add 1 tablespoon of the milk, cover and bring slowly to the boil. Turn off the heat and leave for 10 minutes. Then flake the fish, removing all the skin and any bones. Chop the hard-boiled eggs. Heat remaining milk with the shallot and mace, tip into a jug, cover and leave to infuse. Rinse out the saucepan, melt the butter, blend in the flour, remove from the heat and strain on the milk. Return to the heat, stir until boiling and simmer for 3 minutes, draw pan aside, add the cooked fish and prepared eggs. Then adjust the seasoning. Set oven at 375°F or Mark 5. Fill each pancake with a generous quantity of filling and place in a buttered gratin dish, or dishes. Brush well with melted butter and dust with the grated Parmesan cheese. Put the pancakes into pre-set oven. Bake until brown and crisp (about 7-10 minutes).

Palatschinken

½ pint pancake batter (see page 37)
white sauce (made with 1¼ oz butter,
1 oz plain flour, ¾ pint milk) — see
page 141
2 eggs (separated)
1-2 oz cheese (grated)
salt and pepper

For fillings
choose 3 or 4 from those on the
right to give variety

6-inch diameter cake tin (with re-
movable base)

This recipe, given to Cordon
Bleu many years ago by a
Czechoslovakian, is a marvellous
way of presenting small quantities of leftover meat and vegetables. It is good for a lunch
or supper dish.

Method
Prepare the batter and leave to
stand in a cool place for 30
minutes. Fry pancakes, set
aside and prepare chosen
fillings.
Grease the tin and set oven
at 400°F or Mark 6.
Put alternate layers of pancake and filling into the tin,
beginning and ending with a
pancake.
Prepare the white sauce,
season, draw pan off heat and
beat in the egg yolks, one at
a time. Whip the egg whites
until stiff and fold into the
white sauce with 1 tablespoon
cheese only.
Spoon sauce over the pan-
cakes, making sure that the
sauce runs down the sides.
Sprinkle the top with a thick
layer of grated cheese, set tin on
a baking sheet to catch any
drips and bake in pre-set oven
until brown and crisp (about

20-30 minutes).
Push the 'cake' of pancakes
from the loose-bottomed tin
and slide on to a hot dish with
the help of a palette knife or
fish slice. For serving, cut
pancakes in slices like a cake.

Fillings
Ham. Mix 2-3 oz diced, cooked
ham with 1 teaspoon French
mustard and 1 tablespoon
chutney.

Lamb. Dice 2-3 oz cooked lean
lamb. Cook 1 small sliced onion
in ½ oz butter until golden. Add
the meat, moisten with 1 tablespoon tomato ketchup and 1
tablespoon spicy fruit sauce
and heat the mixture quickly to
boiling point.

Chicken. Dice 2-3 oz cold
cooked chicken and mix with
1 hard-boiled or scrambled egg.
Season well and bind with
a little chicken gravy or cream.

Mushroom. Wash and chop
4 oz mushrooms. Cook 1 finely
chopped shallot in 1 oz butter
until soft, then add the mushrooms and cook until all the
moisture has evaporated. Blend
in 1 teaspoon plain flour and 2-3
tablespoons chicken stock or
milk. Season to taste and bring
mixture to the boil. Then add 1
teaspoon chopped mixed herbs.

Carrot. Heat any leftover
cooked carrots in ½ oz butter
with 1 tablespoon finely chopped onion (you can also add a
little mint sauce).

Gruyère pancakes

Spinach. Leaf or purée spinach may be heated in butter or cream and delicately flavoured with a little grated nutmeg.

Cabbage. Heat 2-3 tablespoons cooked cabbage in butter to drive off any moisture, then flavour with $\frac{1}{2}$ teaspoon paprika pepper, 1 chopped, cooked onion, 1 teaspoon red wine vinegar and a pinch of sugar and dill or caraway seeds. Season well.

Tomato. Melt 1 oz butter and cook 1 finely chopped shallot until soft. Stir in 1 dessertspoon tomato purée, 1 teaspoon paprika pepper, and 4 roughly chopped tomatoes; simmer for 2-3 minutes. Add 2 cold, cooked sausages (sliced) or 2 oz diced Cheddar cheese. Season well and bring quickly to the boil.

For batter
3 $\frac{1}{2}$ oz plain flour
2 eggs
pinch of salt
8-10 fl oz milk and water (mixed)
1 dessertspoon olive oil
1 dessertspoon butter (melted)
1$\frac{3}{4}$ oz Gruyère, or Cheddar, cheese (grated)

For filling
$\frac{3}{4}$ pint thick béchamel sauce (made with 1$\frac{3}{4}$ oz butter, 1$\frac{1}{2}$ oz plain flour, $\frac{3}{4}$ pint flavoured milk) — see page 136
salt and pepper

To finish
1 $\frac{1}{2}$ oz cheese (half Parmesan and half Gruyère, or sharp Cheddar) — grated
$\frac{3}{4}$ oz butter
1 tablespoon chopped parsley

These pancakes can also be made with chopped ham, or mushrooms, or cheese, stirred into the sauce.

Method
Prepare the batter (see page 37), adding the oil, butter and Gruyère cheese when half the liquid has been added. Leave batter to stand for 30 minutes in a cool place.

To prepare filling: make the béchamel sauce and season well. Keep warm.

Set oven at 400°F or Mark 6. Fry the pancakes.

Spread a good tablespoon of sauce on each pancake and roll them up like cigars. Place them in a buttered ovenproof dish and sprinkle with grated cheese. Dot pancakes with butter and brown in oven for about 7-10 minutes. Sprinkle with chopped parsley and serve very hot.

45

Lobster pancakes (Crêpes d'homard)

$\frac{1}{2}$ pint pancake batter (see page 37)

For filling
1 cooked lobster (about 1$\frac{1}{2}$ lb) — see
   page 137, or 2 large cans of lobster
   meat
1 oz butter
1 teaspoon paprika pepper
$\frac{1}{2}$ pint béchamel sauce (see page 136)
1 teaspoon tomato purée
2 tablespoons double cream

For sauce
4 oz button mushrooms
$\frac{1}{2}$ oz butter
1 shallot (finely chopped)
1 onion
2 tablespoons brandy, or dry sherry
$\frac{1}{4}$ pint double cream
salt and pepper
1 tablespoon grated Parmesan
   cheese

Adding the lobster meat to the béchamel sauce with tomato purée before stirring in cream

You can substitute frozen or canned crawfish tails for lobster meat, if preferred.

Method
Prepare batter, leave to stand in a cool place for 30 minutes.

Meanwhile slice the lobster meat from the tail and claws, scoop all the soft meat from the head, or drain canned lobster.

After spreading pancakes with lobster filling, fold them in three, arrange on serving dish

Melt the butter in a pan, add paprika and cook for 1 minute; then put in the tail and claw meat. Set pan aside.

Prepare the béchamel sauce and work in the tomato purée and the creamy meat from the head or canned lobster meat, and simmer for 2-3 minutes. Draw pan aside and stir in the cream, taste for seasoning; keep lobster mixture warm.

Set oven at 350°F or Mark 4. Fry pancakes thinly. Put a table-spoon of lobster mixture on each pancake, fold them in three

Stirring sherry into mushroom sauce; this is poured over pancakes before glazing under grill

and put in a well-buttered oven-proof serving dish in pre-set oven to keep hot.

Wash and trim the mushrooms, slice them finely. Grate onion into a basin, press with a spoon, drain and reserve juice.

Melt butter in a pan, add the shallot and onion juice and cook for 2-3 minutes until shallot is soft but not coloured. Add the mushrooms, increase the heat and cook briskly for 1 minute. Pour on the brandy, or sherry, and cream, season to taste, then boil rapidly for 1 minute.

Pour the sauce over the pan cakes, dust with Parmesan cheese and glaze under the grill. Serve at once.

Cherry pancakes (Crêpes aux cerises)

½ pint pancake batter (see page 37)
1 dessertspoon kirsch

For filling
8 oz black cherries
1 tablespoon kirsch

For topping
caster sugar (for dusting)
1 small carton (2½ fl oz) double cream
pinch of ground cinnamon
2 tablespoon almonds (browned
    and chopped — see page 138)

*Cherry pancakes in cinnamon cream,
with browned chopped almonds*

Method

Prepare the batter (adding the kirsch with the egg) and leave to stand in a cool place for at least 30 minutes.

Meanwhile stone the cherries, pour over 1 tablespoon kirsch, cover and leave for 30 minutes.

Set the oven at 425°F or Mark 7, and fry the pancakes. Put a tablespoon of cherries on each. Roll up pancakes, put them on a baking sheet and dust well with caster sugar. Heat pancakes through in the pre-set oven for 3-4 minutes. Place in a hot serving dish.

Boil the cream with the cinnamon, pour this over the pancakes and scatter the almonds on top. Serve at once.

Creole pancakes

For batter
3 oz plain flour
pinch of salt
2 eggs
5-7½ fl oz milk
1 tablespoon butter (melted), or olive oil
4 tablespoons crushed macaroons
kirsch

For finishing
1 fresh pineapple, or 1 large can
little sugar syrup (see page 140)
2-3 tablespoons apricot jam
kirsch (to taste)
little extra melted butter
icing sugar (for dusting)

Method

Make the batter (see page 37), reserving 1 egg white, and leave in a cool place for about 1 hour. Just before frying pancakes, whisk the egg white until stiff and fold into the batter with the macaroon crumbs and a little kirsch. Fry the pancakes and stack one on top of the other.

Set oven at 425°F or Mark 7. Dice the pineapple, heat quickly in a pan with a little sugar syrup and add the apricot jam and kirsch to taste. Place a tablespoon of pineapple on each pancake, fold them in three and place in a warm buttered ovenproof dish.

Brush pancakes with a little extra melted butter, dust with icing sugar and put into the preset oven for 2-3 minutes.

To serve, pour 2-3 tablespoons kirsch into the hot dish and set it alight.

Pancakes Longueville

For batter
4 oz plain flour
pinch of salt
1 oz caster sugar
1 egg
1 egg yolk
grated rind of 1 orange
2 tablespoons melted butter
scant ½ pint milk
1 oz almonds (freshly blanched and finely chopped) — see page 138

For filling
6 dessert apples (pippin)
grated rind and juice of ½ lemon and ½ orange
4 tablespoons smooth apricot jam
1 small carton (2½ fl oz) double cream
¼ teaspoon cinnamon

To finish
1 tablespoon melted butter
2 tablespoons icing sugar (sifted)

Method

Prepare pancake batter as basic recipe (see page 37), adding grated orange rind with the egg. Leave for 30 minutes in a cool place.

Don't add almonds until just before frying the pancakes.

For filling: peel, quarter and remove the core of the apples and then cut in thick slices. Put in a pan with the lemon and orange rind and juice and the jam, cover and cook until thick and pulpy. Whip the cream and flavour with the cinnamon.

Set oven at 425°F or Mark 7. When pancakes are fried, fold the cream into the apple mixture. Spread each pancake with the mixture, fold in four and place overlapping in a buttered ovenproof dish. Brush with melted butter, dust with icing sugar and glaze in oven for 3-5 minutes. 49

Crêpes Suzette

For batter
3 oz plain flour
pinch of salt
1 egg
1 egg yolk
1 tablespoon olive oil, or 2 tablespoons clarified butter
1 dessertspoon orange curaçao
7½ fl oz milk

For orange butter
6-8 lumps of sugar
2 oranges
2 oz butter (creamed)
1 tablespoon orange curaçao

For serving
little extra melted butter
icing sugar (for dusting)
2-3 tablespoons brandy, or rum (for flaming)

Method

Make the batter (see page 37), adding curaçao at the same time as the eggs and oil or butter. Leave to stand in a cool place for at least 30 minutes before using.

Meanwhile make the orange butter : rub each lump of sugar on the skin of the oranges to remove zest. As you do this the sugar will become saturated with the oil in the zest, and the oranges will look quite bald. Crush the sugar, preferably in a mortar, then work in the creamed butter and curaçao. If you haven't a pestle and mortar, this can be done with the end of your rolling pin in a pudding basin. Keep in a cool place until wanted.

Note : this old-fashioned way of preparing the orange butter is still the very best and perhaps explains why crêpes Suzette are always expensive in a restaurant.

Fry the pancakes as thinly as possible. As the batter is very rich, containing extra butter and liqueur, it is possible to fry them extra thin so that they look quite lacy.

If entertaining at home, the most practical and the simplest way of serving is as follows : set the oven at 300°F or Mark 2, brush a baking tin with a little butter, spread out the pancakes, overlapping each other rather like a pack of cards, and brush with butter. Put pancakes into the pre-set oven for about 5 minutes only.

Have ready a warm serving dish, spread each pancake with orange butter, then fold in three. The folding is traditional — in three like a tricorne (see page 52). Arrange pancakes, overlapping, down the dish and dust with icing sugar. Return them to the oven while the main course is being eaten. Just before carrying the dish to the dining table, heat the brandy or rum in a small pan, set alight and pour over the pancakes.

Removing zest from oranges by rubbing over with sugar lumps

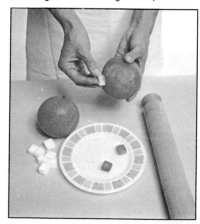

To flame pancakes

If you have a chafing dish and a husband who would love to take over the finishing touch at the dining table, this is what you do to flame pancakes.

Just before serving dinner, unwrap the pancakes you made earlier in the day (it doesn't matter if they are cold) and spread each one with orange butter. (This should be done on the underside, ie. the side fried last, as it never looks as nice and should always become the inside of the filled pancake.)

Stack the pancakes on a plate, put this on a tray with the bottle of brandy or rum, a sherry glass, palette knife, fork, tablespoon and $\frac{1}{2}$ oz unsalted butter. Put this tray beside the chafing dish and have ready a hot serving dish.

Your husband can then carry on as follows : drop butter in the pan and, when foaming, rotate the pan so the whole surface is lightly coated ; put in a pancake, orange butter side down, turn and fold in three ; then lift on to the hot dish.

He should continue in this way until all the pancakes have been heated and turned in their orange butter. By the time the last few pancakes have been heated the sauce should be caramelising on the bottom of the pan — this will give a superb flavour. Then pour the brandy first into the glass and then into the pan. Swill it around pan, tilt and allow brandy to ignite (from the flame). Pour the sauce, while flaming, over the pancakes and serve them at once.

Adding pre-cooked pancake to foaming butter in the chafing dish

Turning and folding pancake before lifting it into the serving dish

Crêpes Suzette (continued)

Crêpes Suzette folded in three, flamed with brandy and set in a serving dish

Apricot pancakes

For batter
4 oz plain flour
pinch of salt
1 egg
1 egg yolk
$\frac{1}{2}$ pint milk
2 tablespoons salad oil, or melted
   butter (for frying)

For filling
1 lb apricots (stoned)
sugar syrup (made with $\frac{1}{2}$ pint water,
   3 rounded tablespoons granulated
   sugar, and pared rind of $\frac{1}{2}$ lemon)
2 tablespoons apricot jam (sieved)
juice of $\frac{1}{2}$ lemon
2 tablespoons almonds
   (flaked and browned, see page
   138) — optional

Method

Prepare batter (see page 37) and leave to stand in a cool place for 30 minutes before using.

Make the sugar syrup and poach the apricots in it (see page 138). Lift the apricots from the pan with a draining spoon, add the jam and lemon juice to the apricot syrup, stir over a gentle heat until the jam has melted, then boil for about 5 minutes until thick and syrupy. Strain.

Set the oven at 400°F or Mark 6, and fry the pancakes.

Layer the pancakes with the apricots in a buttered oven-proof dish, starting and finishing with a pancake. Bake in pre-set oven for about 10 minutes until brown and crisp. Cut like a cake into individual portions and pour over the sauce. Scatter almonds on top and serve hot.

Apricots should be stoned for poaching in syrup, which may be flavoured either with a vanilla pod or with a few pieces of pared lemon rind

Waffle batter (Basic recipe)

8 oz plain flour
1 teaspoon bicarbonate of soda
2 teaspoons baking powder
large pinch of salt
2 eggs
3 oz butter (melted)
¾ pint soured milk, for buttermilk

Waffle iron

This makes about 8 waffles

Method

First heat the waffle iron.

Sift the flour with the bicarbonate of soda, baking powder and salt in a mixing bowl, make a well in the centre and put eggs and melted butter in this. Start adding soured milk to the eggs and whisk gently, or mix with a wooden spoon. Draw in flour very gradually and continue beating until mixture is smooth and all the milk has been added.

Pour mixture from a small jug or spoon into the centre of the hot waffle iron, cover and leave closed until steaming stops. The waffles should be puffed and golden-brown. Serve hot with pats of butter and maple syrup.

Cheese and bacon waffles

Fold 2 oz grated Cheddar cheese into the basic batter. Pour on to the iron and lay thin strips of streaky bacon over the batter before cooking as usual.

Nut waffles

Sprinkle 1 tablespoon roughly chopped browned walnuts over the batter as soon as it is poured on the waffle iron. Serve hot with butter and heather honey.

Bilberry waffles

Cook the waffles in the usual way, then serve them with a thickened compote of bilberries and soured cream or yoghourt.

Make compote by stewing bilberries. Thicken with 1 tablespoon arrowroot slaked with juice of 1 orange.

Hot egg dishes

A hot, tasty and attractively garnished egg dish is ideal for lunch or supper. Not so substantial as a full-blown meat meal, yet pleasantly filling, it is a quick way to eat a nourishing snack.

Many of the dishes we give in this section could also be used as starters for a dinner party. This is the versatility of the egg.

To make these dishes really appetising, follow our basic methods of cooking eggs given on pages 10-14, and prepare your garnish carefully.

Poached eggs écossais

4-5 eggs
1 lb finnan haddock
little milk
2 oz mushrooms
1 oz butter
salt and pepper
4-5 rounds of bread
oil (for frying croûtes)

For sauce
1 oz butter
1 rounded tablespoon plain flour
½ pint milk
2 tablespoons double cream
1 tablespoon grated Parmesan
   cheese
salt and pepper

Method

Poach eggs and keep them in a bowl of warm water.

Trim haddock, put in a shallow pan, cover with cold water, add a dash of milk and bring slowly to the boil. Cover pan, turn off heat and leave for 10 minutes. Then drain fish, remove skin and bone, and flake with a fork ; set aside and keep warm.

Trim, wash and slice mushrooms ; put in a pan with butter and seasoning ready for cooking. Fry bread in hot oil until golden-brown ; drain well.

To prepare sauce : melt butter, stir in flour, blend in milk and bring to the boil. Simmer for 3 minutes, then beat in cream and cheese. Season to taste.

Place croûtes in a hot gratin dish, toss prepared mushrooms over a quick flame for about 1 minute and mix in haddock. Drain the eggs, arrange on the croûtes and scatter haddock and mushroom mixture on top. Spoon over the sauce and glaze under grill for 2-3 minutes.

Eggs beurre noir

(with black butter)

4-5 eggs
4 pieces of bread for croûtes, or 4
   slices of buttered toast
2 oz butter
parsley (freshly chopped)
salt and pepper
1 dessertspoon chopped gherkins
1 dessertspoon capers
2 tablespoons wine vinegar

A quick and delicious way of serving poached eggs. The acidulated yet buttery sauce makes a good contrast.

Method

Poach the eggs and keep them in hot water.

Fry the bread for croûtes in a little extra butter.

Drain eggs well and place each one on a croûte or buttered toast. Set in a hot dish.

Heat a frying pan, drop in the butter and cook to a deep nut-brown. Quickly add the parsley, seasoning, gherkins and capers, and pour at once over the eggs. Add the vinegar to the pan, boil to reduce by half, and sprinkle it over the eggs.

Serve with boiled potatoes and green salad.

Eggs with ham

5 eggs
3-4 oz macaroni
½ oz butter
5 thin slices of cooked ham
grated cheese (for sprinkling)

For béchamel sauce
1 oz butter
1 oz plain flour
¾ pint milk (infused with 1 slice of onion, bouquet garni, 6 pepper-corns)
salt and pepper

This recipe, using soft-boiled eggs, makes a substantial supper dish.

Method
Softboil the eggs and put into cold water.

Meanwhile cook the maca-roni in plenty of boiling salted water until tender (about 15-20 minutes), drain, refresh and return to the pan with ½ oz butter. Reheat and put into the bottom of a well-buttered gratin or ovenproof dish and keep hot.

To prepare béchamel sauce: melt butter in a pan, remove from the heat, blend in the flour and strain on the milk. Stir over gentle heat until boiling, season to taste, and then cook for 2-3 minutes.

Peel eggs, wrap each in a slice of ham and arrange on the macaroni. Spoon over the béchamel sauce, sprinkle with grated cheese and brown lightly under the grill, or in a hot oven at 400°F or Mark 6 for about 10 minutes.

Eggs mexicaine

5 eggs (new-laid)
2 onions (finely chopped)
2 oz butter
1 large green pepper (diced and blanched)
1 large can, or 1 large packet of frozen, sweetcorn kernels
1 rounded tablespoon tomato chutney, or pickle
salt and pepper

For sauce
1 oz butter
1 rounded tablespoon plain flour
7½ fl oz milk
2½ fl oz double cream
3 oz cheese (grated)

Method
Poach or softboil the eggs, peel and keep in warm water. Sauté the chopped onion in 1 oz butter until turning colour, add the pepper and the corn, drained if from a can, or blanched if frozen. Add remaining butter and the chutney or pickle. Season well and shake up over the heat until very hot. Then set aside.

To prepare sauce: melt butter in pan, stir in flour and pour on the milk, blend and bring to the boil. Remove from heat. Add the cream and the cheese, a little at a time. Reserve a little cheese for the top of the dish.

Turn the corn mixture into an ovenproof dish, arrange the well drained eggs on top and coat with sauce. Sprinkle on the rest of the cheese and brown under the grill.

Eggs soubise

5-6 eggs
2 Spanish onions
little egg white
seasoned plain flour
deep fat (for frying)

For soubise sauce
½ lb onions (chopped)
1¾ oz butter
1 rounded tablespoon plain flour
¾ pint milk

One of the best hot egg dishes. The creamy sauce contrasts well with the crisp brown onions.

Method
First make soubise sauce : blanch chopped onions, drain well and simmer in 1 oz butter until soft but not brown. Mix in an electric blender or rub through a strainer. Melt remaining butter in a pan ; add flour, then milk, and stir until boiling. Then add the onion purée and cook for 4-5 minutes until creamy ; keep hot.

Slice Spanish onions and push out into rings, moisten with a little raw egg white and dust well with seasoned flour until they are dry. Fry in deep fat, keep hot.

Poach eggs and drain well. Arrange them in a dish, coat with the sauce and arrange the onion rings around them.

Left : moisten onion rings with egg white, dust dry with seasoned flour ; fry in deep fat, being sure not to crowd the pan
Below : to finish, drain onion rings well and arrange at the sides of the egg and onion sauce mixture

Eggs Bénédictine

5 eggs
scant 1 oz butter
1 clove of garlic (crushed with
$\frac{1}{2}$ teaspoon salt)
1 lb cooked fresh haddock
(flaked), or other white fish
$\frac{1}{4}$ pint white sauce (made with $\frac{1}{2}$ oz
butter, $\frac{1}{2}$ oz plain flour, $\frac{1}{4}$ pint milk)
— see page 141
2 $\frac{1}{2}$ tablespoons single cream, or
creamy milk

For cream sauce
$\frac{3}{4}$ oz butter
1 tablespoon plain flour
7 $\frac{1}{2}$ fl oz milk plus 2 $\frac{1}{2}$ fl oz single
cream, or $\frac{1}{2}$ pint milk

To garnish
1 French roll (sliced) — for croûtes
oil, or butter (for frying)

Method
Softboil eggs, peel and put
in warm water.

Melt butter in pan, add
crushed garlic, cook for 1
minute, then add fish. Work
over a low heat, adding the
white sauce gradually. Stir in
cream. Spread on the bottom
of a serving dish, drain eggs
and arrange on the fish.

To make cream sauce: melt
butter in pan, stir in flour off the
heat, stir in milk and bring to
the boil. Remove pan from heat
and add cream (if using).

To make croûtes : fry slices of
French roll in fat until brown
and crisp, drain on absorbent
paper.

Coat eggs with the cream
sauce, or use a mornay sauce
if preferred (see page 138) ;
serve immediately, garnished
with croûtes.

Eggs Suzette

5 small eggs (new-laid)
5 large potatoes
salt
4 oz mushrooms (sliced)
1$\frac{1}{4}$ oz butter
1 teaspoon plain flour
2-3 tablespoons stock (see page 139)
4 oz cooked ham (sliced and
shredded)
2 tablespoons hot milk
grated cheese

For mornay sauce
$\frac{1}{2}$ oz butter
$\frac{1}{2}$ oz plain flour
$\frac{1}{4}$ pint milk
1 oz cheese (grated)

Method
Clean potatoes, but do not peel,
roll them in salt and bake in
oven at 350°F or Mark 4 for
about 1$\frac{1}{2}$ hours or until tender.

Sauté the sliced mushrooms
in about $\frac{1}{2}$ oz butter in a small
pan, then dust with flour.
Moisten with the stock, bring
to the boil, add the ham and set
aside. Make the mornay sauce
(see method, page 138) and
poach or softboil the eggs.

Cut off tops of the potatoes
(lengthways) and carefully
scoop out the pulp. Put this
into a warm basin and mash
thoroughly. Add $\frac{1}{2}$ oz butter and
hot milk to make a purée.

Put a spoonful of the mushroom and ham mixture into the
bottom of each potato, place a
well-drained egg on top and
coat with the mornay sauce.
Top with the purée of potato or
put into a forcing bag, with a
vegetable rose pipe, and pipe
potato to cover the eggs completely. Sprinkle with grated
cheese and brown under grill.

Eggs 'en surprise'

4-5 new-laid eggs

For soufflé mixture
2 lb spinach
1½ oz butter
scant 1 oz plain flour
¼ pint creamy milk
grated nutmeg
salt and pepper
3 egg yolks
2 oz cooked ham (chopped) —
optional
4 egg whites
a little grated Parmesan cheese
mixed with browned crumbs (see
page 29)

4-5 individual soufflé dishes

Method

Softboil the eggs; peel and keep in cold water.

Wash spinach thoroughly, cook in a pan of salted boiling water, refresh and drain well. Rub through a sieve or work in an electric blender.

Prepare soufflé mixture; melt ½ oz butter in a medium-size pan, cook to a noisette (nut brown), then add spinach purée and cook over a steady heat to drive away any excess liquid. Blend in the remaining butter, the flour and milk, add the grated nutmeg, season and stir until just boiling. Cool slightly and beat in the yolks, one at a time. (Add chopped ham.)

Whip the egg whites to a firm snow and stir 2 tablespoons into the spinach mixture to soften the mixture a little, then quickly fold in the remainder. Well butter the dishes and put a layer of the soufflé mixture in bottom of each one.

Drain and dry the eggs and put one in each dish. Cover with rest of the mixture. Dust the top with grated cheese and browned crumbs mixed together and bake in oven pre-set at 400°F or Mark 6 for 20-25 minutes. Serve at once.

As an alternative to the spinach, use a plain cheese soufflé mixture (see page 29).

Convent eggs

4-5 eggs (new-laid)
salt and pepper
1 small carton (2 ½ fl oz) double
cream, or 1 tablespoon per egg
1 oz butter

4-5 individual cocottes

This simple dish may be cooked in a large ovenproof dish instead of individual cocottes.

Tomato sauce may be used instead of the cream, with shredded ham, chicken, or sauté sliced chicken liver, placed in the cocottes under the eggs.

Method

Set oven at 350°F or Mark 4. Butter the dish or cocottes. Break each egg into a cup and slide it carefully into chosen dish. Season eggs and spoon over the cream. Set dish or cocottes on a baking sheet and cook in the pre-set oven for 7-8 minutes, until the whites are jellied and the yolks barely set.

Convent eggs are topped with cream before baking in individual cocottes

Eggs à la crème with mushrooms

5-6 eggs
3 oz mushrooms (sliced)
$\frac{1}{2}$ oz butter
squeeze of lemon juice
$\frac{1}{4}$ pint double cream
salt and pepper
pinch of grated nutmeg
3 oz Gruyère cheese (grated)

5-6 ramekins

This makes a very good party dish.

Method
Set oven at 350°F or Mark 4. Cook the sliced mushrooms very quickly in the butter with a squeeze of lemon. Pour half the cream into the ramekins, break the eggs carefully on top and then cover with the mushrooms.

Season the remaining cream, add grated nutmeg, and spoon it over the mushrooms. Cover each ramekin with a thick layer of grated Gruyère cheese, stand in a bain-marie of very hot water and cook in pre-set oven for 10 minutes. Serve hot.

Eggs flamenco

4-5 eggs
2 potatoes
2 oz butter
2 frankfurters, or smoked sausages, or saveloys (sliced)
salt and pepper
2 tablespoons peas (cooked)
2 fresh, or canned, sweet red peppers (cut into shreds)
8 tomatoes (skinned, quartered and seeds removed) — see page 141
chopped parsley
2 tablespoons top of milk, or single cream
cayenne pepper

Method
Peel potatoes, cover with cold water and bring to boil. Cook for 4 minutes, strain and dice.

Set oven at 350°F or Mark 4.

Melt the butter in a pan, add the potatoes and sausages. Shake pan over the heat until the potatoes begin to brown; season, add peas and sweet peppers. After 4-5 minutes add the tomatoes and a good sprinkling of parsley.

Turn the mixture into the bottom of a flat ovenproof dish, and break the eggs on top. Season again, pour milk or cream on top and place in pre-set oven for 6 minutes, or until set.

Sprinkle each egg with a little cayenne pepper to serve.

Eggs savoyarde

5 eggs
1 oz butter
1 gammon rasher (about 3 oz)
— cut in strips
1 small head of celeriac, or
½ large one (sliced)
1 small onion (sliced)
2 medium-size potatoes (sliced)
salt and pepper
4 tablespoons double cream
grated cheese (preferably
Gruyère)

This dish is a good way of using root celery (celeriac). The bacon can be omitted but gives a good savoury taste to the dish.

Method
Melt butter in a shallow pan, put in the bacon strips and, after 1-2 minutes, the sliced vegetables. Season and cover with a close-fitting lid. Cook gently until the vegetables are tender but not coloured.

Set oven at 350°F or Mark 4.

Spread this mixture over the base of an ovenproof dish. Break the eggs on top, spoon over the cream and put the grated cheese on top. Cook in pre-set oven for 8-10 minutes.

Eggs portugaise

4 eggs (hard-boiled)
½-¾ lb tomatoes (skinned and
sliced) — see page 141
2 oz butter
1 tablespoon finely chopped mixed
herbs
salt and pepper
grated cheese

For sauce
¾ oz butter
1 rounded tablespoon plain flour
½ pint milk (infused with 1 slice of
onion, 1 carrot, bouquet garni,
6 peppercorns)
salt

Portugaise usually describes a dish in which tomato is used.

Method
Sauté the prepared tomatoes for 1-2 minutes in ½ oz butter. Cut eggs in half lengthways. Sieve yolks, cream remaining butter and mix with sieved yolks, herbs and seasoning to taste. Fill the egg whites with this mixture and arrange on tomatoes in an ovenproof dish.

Set oven at 425°F or Mark 7.

To prepare sauce: melt the butter in a pan, draw aside and stir in the flour. Strain on the infused milk, return to the heat and stir until boiling. Season to taste and simmer for 2-3 minutes.

Coat the eggs with the sauce, sprinkle with grated cheese and brown in pre-set oven.

Hungarian eggs

5 eggs (hard-boiled and sliced)
4 small onions (thinly sliced)
little butter (for frying)
½ lb tomatoes (skinned and
  sliced with seeds removed)
paprika pepper
about 1 oz tomato butter (to
  garnish) — see below

This is an easy and quick dish
to make; and the tomato butter
gives it an unusual touch.

Method
Fry the sliced onions in the
butter until golden-brown. Add
the prepared tomatoes and
simmer for 4-5 minutes.

Put the sliced eggs in the
serving dish, cover with the
tomato mixture and dust with
paprika. Garnish the top with
round flat pats of tomato butter.

Tomato butter

Work together 1 oz or more
of butter 1 teaspoon tomato
purée, salt and pepper and
2-3 drops of Worcestershire
sauce. Chill and shape into
pats each about the size of
a ten new penny piece.

Eggs à la tripe

4-5 eggs (hard-boiled)
½ lb onions, or preferably spring
  onions
1 oz butter
salt and pepper

For béchamel sauce
¾ pint milk (infused with 4-5 parsley
  stalks, 6 peppercorns, 1 blade of
  mace and 1 bayleaf)
1 oz butter
2 tablespoons plain flour
salt and pepper
grated cheese

This dish is so called because
of the way the egg whites are
cut, resembling shreds of tripe.

Method
Cut the eggs in half and push
out the yolks. Wash whites and
cut into shreds. Rub the yolks
through a sieve. Keep whites
and yolks in separate small
basins, well covered.

Cut spring onions into 2-3
pieces, or thinly slice ordinary
ones. Put them into a pan of
cold water, bring to the boil and
strain. Return to the pan with
1 oz butter; season, cover and
simmer gently until just tender
(about 7-8 minutes).

Set oven at 400°F or Mark 6.
Meanwhile prepare the sauce:
strain infused milk and leave
to cool. Melt butter in a pan,
remove from heat and stir in
flour. Pour on milk, stir over
moderate heat until boiling,
then boil until thick and creamy.
Season.

Butter an ovenproof dish, put
in the egg whites, scatter on the
onions, then the sieved yolks.
Spoon sauce over the top,
sprinkle with grated cheese and
brown in pre-set oven for 7-10
minutes.

Eggs cantalienne

4 large eggs (hard-boiled)
1 small cabbage
2 oz butter
1 wineglass white wine, or stock
    (see page 139)
salt and pepper
2 shallots (finely chopped)
browned crumbs (see page 29)

For sauce
1 oz butter
1 rounded tablespoon plain flour
½ pint milk
½ teaspoon French mustard
1½ oz cheese (grated)

> **Cantal** is a cheese of the Auvergne district of France, made from a mixture of cow's, ewe's and goat's milk. Grated Cheddar cheese is also suitable for eggs cantalienne.

Method

Cut the cabbage in quarters, remove the hard stalk and shred leaves finely. Blanch in pan of boiling salted water for 1 minute, drain and return to the pan with 1 oz butter and wine or stock. Season, cover with buttered paper and the lid and simmer for 5-6 minutes until the cabbage is just tender.

Meanwhile prepare the sauce : melt 1 oz butter in a pan, add flour and blend in half the milk. Stir until boiling, draw aside and mix in mustard and three-quarters of the cheese.

Cook the chopped shallots slowly in the remaining 1 oz butter until soft.

Split the eggs lengthways. Remove the yolks, rub them through a wire sieve and mix with the shallots and 2 tablespoons sauce. Fill the whites as fully as possible with the mixture. Add the rest of the milk to the sauce and reheat.

Dish up the cabbage and lay down the centre of a hot serving dish, arrange the eggs on top and spoon over the sauce. Sprinkle with browned crumbs mixed with remaining grated cheese and brown under grill or in oven at 400°F or Mark 6 for 10 minutes.

Eggs gascon

5 eggs
1 medium-size onion (thinly
  sliced)
4-5 tablespoons oil
1-2 aubergines (according to
  size) — sliced and dégorgé
$\frac{1}{2}$ lb tomatoes (skinned and
  thickly sliced) — see page 141
salt and pepper
dripping, or oil (for frying eggs)
2 gammon rashers (shredded)

Method

Sauté onion slices in the oil until just brown. Take them out. Dry the aubergine slices and place them in the pan. Sauté in the oil until golden-brown. Pour off any surplus fat and add the sliced tomatoes. Season, put back onion and cook for 6-7 minutes until mixture is rich and pulpy. Turn into a hot serving dish and keep warm.

Wipe out pan, heat fat (or oil) and fry the eggs. Then place on top of the aubergine mixture. Shred the gammon and fry for 3-4 minutes in the pan. Scatter over the eggs and serve at once.

Eggs gascon — a substantial lunch dish of fried eggs with gammon rashers, aubergines, onion and tomatoes, served very hot

Eggs romaine

5 eggs
1-1½ lb spinach
1 oz butter
fat (for frying)
salt and pepper
anchovy fillets, or 1 rasher of
   bacon (to garnish)
cream sauce (see below)

This is a good way of serving fried eggs as a main course.

Method
Wash and cook the spinach in plenty of boiling salted water, drain thoroughly and chop finely, or leave 'en branche' (in leaves).
Put butter in pan and cook gently to a noisette (nut-brown). Add spinach and cook it quickly to drive off any moisture. Fry the eggs in deep fat, drain and sprinkle them with salt and pepper.
Dish up spinach on a serving dish and arrange eggs on top. Garnish with the anchovy fillets, split in two, or a curl of fried bacon.
Serve a light cream sauce separately.

> **A light cream sauce** is easily made by heating a little single cream, seasoning with salt, pepper and a squeeze of lemon juice.

Eggs en cocotte

4-5 new-laid eggs
8-15 small slices of Gruyère
   cheese
salt and pepper
4-5 tablespoons double cream
paprika pepper

Chafing dish ; 4-5 individual cocottes

Though any recipes for baked eggs (en cocotte) are suitable for cooking in a chafing dish, this one is particularly good.

Method
Half fill the chafing dish with boiling salted water. Butter the cocottes well and put 2-3 small slices of cheese in the bottom of each. Break in the eggs, season and add 1 tablespoon cream to each cocotte. Dust with paprika, stand the cocottes in the water (let water come just up to rims), cover with a lid and cook very slowly for 7-8 minutes until the eggs are just setting.

Buttered eggs with asparagus

8 eggs (2 per person)
salt and pepper
4 oz butter
2 tablespoons double cream
bundle of asparagus, or sprue

For croûtons
4-6 slices of stale bread
1 oz butter (for frying)

Method
Break eggs into a bowl, beat up with a fork and season.
Prepare croûtons : cut the stale bread into small dice and fry in about 1 oz of butter and set aside.
Melt $1\frac{1}{2}$ oz of the butter in pan, add about two-thirds of the egg mixture and cook slightly until thick and creamy. Then add the rest of the eggs, the butter and cream. Stir until really thick, then put into a hot dish.
Surround with fried croûtons and asparagus, trimmed and cooked in small bundles.

Simple egg curry

4 eggs
2 oz butter
1 large onion (finely sliced)
2 teaspoons curry powder
$\frac{1}{4}$ teaspoon ground ginger
$\frac{1}{4}$ green pepper (seeded and chopped)
salt
1 tablespoon lemon juice, or
1 dessertspoon lime juice
$\frac{1}{2}$ pint water

Method
Hardboil the eggs, shell and halve them. Heat the butter and fry the onion until lightly browned. Add the spices and cook gently for 1-2 minutes. then stir in the chopped green pepper and $\frac{1}{4}$ teaspoon salt. Add the water, blend in and stir until the sauce has thickened, Add the lemon or lime juice and put in the eggs, cut surface down. Spoon the sauce over them and leave about 10 minutes for the eggs to heat through before serving.
Serve with freshly boiled rice (see method, page 101).

Egg and mushroom, or prawn, bouchées

8 oz quantity of puff pastry (see page 138)
egg wash (made with 1 egg beaten with $\frac{1}{2}$ teaspoon salt)

For filling
$\frac{1}{4}$ lb mushrooms (quartered, or sliced) and 4 eggs (hard-boiled and coarsely chopped), or 4-5 oz prawns (shelled and chopped)
1$\frac{1}{2}$ oz butter
1 rounded tablespoon plain flour
$\frac{1}{2}$ pint milk (infused with 1 slice of onion, $\frac{1}{2}$ bayleaf, 6 peppercorns)
salt and pepper

2$\frac{1}{2}$-inch diameter fluted cutter, 1$\frac{1}{2}$-inch diameter cutter (fluted, or plain)

The bouchée cases can be made the same day or a few days beforehand and stored in an airtight container. This filling is sufficient for 6-8 bouchées.

Method
Set oven at 425°F or Mark 7. Roll out made pastry to just over $\frac{1}{4}$-inch thickness and stamp it out into bouchées 2$\frac{1}{2}$ inches in diameter. Set on a dampened baking sheet and brush with egg wash. Make circular incisions with the smaller cutter to form lids. Bake in pre-set oven for 15-20 minutes until golden-brown.

If using eggs and mushrooms, continue as follows : trim mushrooms, wash them quickly, drain and quarter or slice them depending on their size. Melt half the butter, add the mushrooms and sauté them for 2-3 minutes. Draw pan off the heat and add the remaining butter (the heat of the pan will melt it automatically) and blend in the flour and strained, flavoured milk. Season and stir sauce until boiling ; cook for 2-3 minutes, then add the chopped eggs.

If using prawns, make sauce with butter, flour and drained milk. Stir in prawns.

Remove lids and fill bouchées with the mixture. Replace lids and reheat a few minutes in oven before serving very hot.

If you have baked bouchées a few days before, the best way to reheat them is as follows : first set oven at 350°F or Mark 4. Fill cold bouchées with hot filling and heat for 10 minutes.

Cream of tunny fish and egg

1-2 cans tunny fish, according
  to size
4 hard-boiled eggs
1 tablespoon browned breadcrumbs (see page 29) and grated
  cheese (mixed together)

For sauce
2 oz onions (finely sliced)
1½ oz butter
¾ oz plain flour
½-¾ pint milk
salt and pepper
2 oz cheese (grated)

Pie dish (1-1½ pints capacity)

Method
First prepare the sauce. Soften
onion in half the butter, add the
remainder and stir in the flour.
Pour on the milk, stir until
boiling, season, then draw aside
and beat in the cheese by
degrees, reserving a little for
the top.
  Pour a little sauce into an
ovenproof dish, flake the tunny
fish and arrange on top with the
sliced or halved eggs. Coat
with the rest of the sauce.
Scatter with crumbs and cheese
and brown in a quick oven, at
450°F or Mark 8, or under grill.

Banana and egg dish

6 bananas
6 eggs
2 medium-size onions (finely
  sliced)
1 oz butter
2 tomatoes (skinned and
  chopped)
1 green chilli (seeded and finely
  chopped)
1 tablespoon chopped coriander
  leaves
½ teaspoon ground turmeric
1 clove of garlic (crushed with
  salt)
salt

Method
Set oven at 350°F or Mark 4.
Fry the onions in the butter
until brown. Peel and slice the
bananas about ½ inch thick,
add to the pan with all the
other ingredients, except the
eggs, and cook gently until the
bananas are soft. Turn into a
shallow ovenproof dish and
make 6 hollows in the mixture.
Break the eggs into these and
bake in pre-set oven for 10-15
minutes, or until eggs are set.

*Breaking eggs into hollows in ba-
nana, tomato, herb and spice mixture
for banana and egg dish*

Eggs Jacqueline

4 eggs
1½ oz butter
½ teaspoon paprika pepper
6 oz shelled prawns
salt and pepper
1 packet (about 12 oz) frozen
   asparagus
½ pint béchamel sauce (see page 136)

To finish
1 tablespoon grated Parmesan
cheese

Method
Hardboil the eggs and cut them in two lengthways. Sieve the yolks and place the whites in a bowl of cold water. Cream the butter with the paprika and mix with the yolks, adding 2 oz of the prawns, finely chopped. Season to taste. Cook the asparagus following the instructions on the packet, drain, refresh it with cold water to set the colour and drain again.

Set oven at 400°F or Mark 6.

Prepare the béchamel sauce, season to taste and simmer for 2-3 minutes. Place the asparagus in a buttered ovenproof dish, fill the egg whites with the prawn mixture and place on the asparagus. Scatter the remaining prawns (whole) on top. Coat the filled eggs with the béchamel sauce, sprinkle with the cheese and bake in pre-set oven for 15-20 minutes until golden-brown.

Eggs Jacqueline make an unusual but delicious starter to a meal

Eggs florentine

6 eggs (new-laid)
1½ lb spinach
½ oz butter
salt and pepper

For mornay sauce
1½ oz butter
1¼ oz plain flour
½-¾ pint milk
2 oz Cheddar, or Cheshire,
    cheese (grated)
salt and pepper
little made English mustard

Method
Poach the eggs and leave in cold water until wanted. Boil the spinach, drain and press. Then return to the pan with $\frac{1}{2}$ oz butter and season. Shake pan over the heat for 1-2 minutes, then arrange spinach down the centre of an ovenproof dish; drain and dry the eggs and place on top.

Prepare mornay sauce (see method, page 138). Allow to boil well, then draw pan aside before adding 1½ oz of the cheese. Season the sauce well and coat the eggs with it. Sprinkle with the rest of cheese and brown under the grill, or in a quick oven at 425°F or Mark 7, for 5-6 minutes.

Devilled anchovy eggs

6 soft-boiled eggs (peeled)
1-2 oz butter
scant teaspoon made English
    mustard
2 tablespoons tomato sauce (see
    page 140)
1 tablespoon Worcestershire sauce
1 tablespoon mushroom ketchup
salt and pepper
4 rounds of toast (well buttered and
    spread with Gentleman's Relish,
    or anchovy paste)

Chafing dish

This recipe was recommended in an old cookery book as a pick-me-up for breakfast after an evening's indulgence. Apparently it is the anchovy paste that does the trick, especially if it is spread on hot buttered toast.

Method
Put the butter, mustard and sauces in the chafing dish; mix well. When simmering, add the peeled eggs and seasoning, using a potato masher to break them, and mix them well with the devilled mixture. When just at the point of setting, and thoroughly hot, turn on to the toast and serve at once.

Cauliflower snow (Choufleur à la neige)

1 large cauliflower
1 large onion (sliced)
1 oz butter
2 tomatoes (scalded, skinned and sliced) — see page 141
4 eggs (separated)
2 oz Cheddar cheese (grated)

For mornay sauce
1 oz butter
1 oz plain flour
½ pint milk
salt and pepper
4 oz Cheddar cheese (grated)

Method
Cut cauliflower into fleurettes and cook in boiling salted water, stems down, for 5-10 minutes. Sauté the onion in butter until soft, add tomatoes and cook for 2-3 minutes.

Make the sauce (see page 138). Arrange in a gratin dish, spoon over the onion and tomato mixture and coat with sauce.

Beat the egg whites stiffly and arrange on top of cauliflower, making four pockets for the egg yolks. Drop a yolk into each pocket. Sprinkle over the remaining cheese and grill until crisp and golden-brown.

Eggs Chimay

5 eggs
seasoned plain flour
beaten egg
dried white breadcrumbs
fried parsley (optional)
7½ fl oz well-reduced tomato sauce
(for serving) — see page 140

For filling
1 small onion
1 oz butter
6 oz flat mushrooms
1 oz plain flour
about 3-4 fl oz stock, or milk
1 dessertspoon chopped fresh
herbs, or pinch of dried herbs
with a little fresh parsley
salt and pepper
1 egg yolk

Deep fat bath

Method
Hardboil the eggs and then leave to cool. Meanwhile prepare filling: chop onion finely and soften in a pan with the butter. Chop mushrooms, without peeling or removing stalks, then add them to the pan. Cook fairly briskly, stirring frequently, until much of the moisture has been driven off. Draw pan aside, stir in the flour and add the stock (or milk). Replace on heat, stir until boiling, then draw pan aside and add herbs and seasoning.

Peel the cooled eggs and cut carefully in half lengthways. Scoop out yolks, rub them through a strainer and mix into the mushroom mixture; add the raw yolk. The mixture must be stiff but not too dry. Well wash and dry halved egg whites. Fill each half with the mushroom mixture and join them together again to form a whole egg. Roll them in seasoned flour, then in the egg and crumbs, and fry in deep fat until golden-brown. Drain well and dish up. Garnish, if wished, with fried parsley. Heat the tomato sauce and serve separately.

If more convenient, these eggs may be deep-fried a little while before serving, then reheated in a hot oven (400°F or Mark 6) for about 5 minutes.

Filling halved egg whites with the mushroom mixture before reshaping

Eggs Xérès

6 large eggs
2 medium-size carrots
2 $\frac{1}{2}$ oz butter
1 glass golden sherry
salt and pepper
grated rind and $\frac{1}{2}$ juice of 1 small
   orange
2 tablespoons double cream

To garnish
watercress — optional

This rather unusual recipe is good for a summer lunch.

Xérès is the ancient name for Jerez in Spain, the home of sherry.

These ingredients are used in eggs Xérès — it is from the sherry that the dish gets its name

Method
Peel carrots, slice thinly lengthways, then cut across into needle-like shreds.

Melt $\frac{1}{2}$ oz butter in a small pan, put in carrots and, after 2-3 minutes gentle cooking, add the sherry. Season, cover tightly and continue to cook until tender and the sherry has almost disappeared (about 5 minutes). Draw pan aside, add the orange rind and juice.

Break the eggs, beat with a fork until frothy, then season and add the cream. Add the carrot mixture to the eggs. Melt the remaining butter in a fairly large pan, pour in egg mixture and stir slowly until creamy. Then put in a hot dish, garnish with watercress, serve at once.

Cold egg dishes

These are probably the most unusual of all egg dishes, for few people can keep eggs tasting good after they have gone cold. The secret, of course, is in not just letting them cool off after cooking. You must take steps to cool the egg quickly once it is cooked, so that it doesn't go on cooking in its own heat.

Once mastered, this art produces some of the most delicious starters and light lunch and supper dishes — so follow our basic methods section for tips.

Eggs Connaught

6 hard-boiled eggs
$\frac{1}{4}$ pint milk
1 slice of onion
blade of mace
6 peppercorns
$3\frac{1}{2}$ oz butter
1 tablespoon plain flour
salt and pepper
1 packet Demi-sel cheese
1 teaspoon paprika pepper
4 oz prawns (shelled)
$\frac{1}{2}$ bunch of watercress (to garnish)

Method

Scald the milk with the onion, mace and peppercorns, tip into a jug, cover and leave to infuse. Rinse the pan with cold water, drop in $\frac{1}{2}$ oz butter, heat gently and blend in the flour. Strain on the milk and add salt. Stir continuously, bring milk to the boil, cook 1 minute. Turn on to a plate, cover with buttered paper to prevent a skin forming and leave sauce until cold. Cream remaining butter until soft.

Split the hard-boiled eggs in two, scoop out the yolks and rub through a wire strainer; keep the whites in a bowl of water as they soon get hard if exposed to air. Work the yolks with the butter, cheese, paprika and cold sauce. Chop half the prawns finely, add to the mixture and season to taste. Drain and dry the egg whites and have ready a round serving dish or use a cake platter.

Spoon a drop of filling on to the dish to hold each egg white in position, arrange them in a circle and then fill each with the mixture, or you can use a piping bag with a $\frac{1}{2}$-inch plain nozzle. Scatter over the remaining prawns (split in half, if large) and dust with paprika. Place the watercress in the middle and serve brown bread and butter separately.

Prawn and egg mousse

8 oz prawns (frozen, or fresh) — peeled and very finely chopped
12 eggs (hard-boiled and peeled)
¾ pint mayonnaise (see page 137)
2 egg whites
1 ½ oz gelatine (see page 137)
¼ pint stock, or wine, or water
salt and pepper

For béchamel sauce
2 oz butter
2 oz plain flour
1 pint milk (flavoured with 1 teaspoon paprika pepper and 1 teaspoon tomato purée)

For devilled garnish
1 lb tomatoes
8 oz prawns (frozen, or fresh) — peeled
2-3 drops of Tabasco sauce
1 teaspoon tomato ketchup
3 tablespoons French dressing (see page 136)

small cress, or cucumber, or watercress and extra slices of tomato

Ring mould (2¼ pints capacity)

Method
First oil the mould, then divide the hard-boiled eggs in half, remove the yolks and rub them through a wire strainer; chop the egg whites.

Prepare the béchamel sauce (see page 136) and, when cold, pound with the prawns and sieved egg yolks until smooth, then work in the mayonnaise.

Stiffly whip the egg whites; dissolve the gelatine in the stock (or wine or water) and add to the mayonnaise mixture with the chopped egg whites and season well. As the mixture begins to thicken, fold in the egg whites. Turn mousse into the oiled mould and leave to set (about 2 hours).

Prepare the garnish. Scald and skin the tomatoes and cut them into four. Remove the hard core and the seeds, then cut the flesh into fine shreds. Add the Tabasco sauce and tomato ketchup to the French dressing and mix this with the tomatoes and prawns.

When the mousse is set, turn it out on a large dish and fill the centre with the devilled tomatoes and prawns. Garnish the dish with a salad of your choice: small cress, cucumber, watercress and extra slices of tomato.

Above : pounding béchamel with prawns and sieved yolks
Below : garnishing prawn and egg mousse with the watercress

Eggs mollets à l'indienne

5 eggs
4 oz long grain rice (boiled, drained and dried — see page 101)
2-3 tablespoons French dressing (see page 136)
½ pint thick mayonnaise (see page 137)
salt and pepper

To garnish
pimiento (shredded)
watercress

For curry mixture
1 shallot (finely chopped)
1 tablespoon oil
1 dessertspoon curry powder
1 teaspoon paprika pepper
1 teaspoon tomato purée (diluted with ½ cup of water), or ½ cup of tomato juice
2 slices of lemon
1 dessertspoon apricot jam

Method

First prepare the curry mixture : soften the shallot in oil, add curry powder and paprika and after 3-4 seconds the remaining ingredients. Stir well and simmer for 4-5 minutes. Strain and set mixture aside.

Softboil or poach the eggs. Moisten the rice with a little French dressing ; arrange down the centre of a serving dish.

Add enough of the curry mixture to the mayonnaise to flavour it well. Adjust seasoning and spoon curry mayonnaise over the eggs. Garnish with the pimiento and watercress.

> A l'indienne means, literally, in Indian style. The term is usually applied to dishes that contain either curry or chutney, or both, accompanied by a dish of plain boiled rice.

Eggs mollets à l'indienne — in a curry mayonnaise, garnished with pimiento and watercress

Egg à la grecque

6 eggs
6 oz smoked cod's roe
2 oz unsalted butter
squeeze of lemon juice
$\frac{1}{2}$ oz gelatine (see page 137)
8 tablespoons tomato juice

For $\frac{1}{2}$ pint mayonnaise
2 egg yolks
salt and pepper
dry mustard
$\frac{3}{4}$ cup of salad oil
2 tablespoons wine vinegar

For tomato salad
1 lb tomatoes
$\frac{1}{2}$ teaspoon caster sugar

For French dressing
4 tablespoons salad oil
salt
black pepper (ground from mill)
juice and rind of $\frac{1}{2}$ lemon

Method

Hardboil the eggs, shell and keep them in cold water.

Prepare the mayonnaise (see method, page 137).

Remove skin from cod's roe. Work butter in a bowl until soft, with a wooden spoon. Cut eggs in half lengthways, remove yolks and push through a wire strainer. Pound the roe, butter and egg yolks together, adding lemon juice and 1-2 tablespoons of mayonnaise to make a creamy consistency. Fill egg whites, reshape each egg and arrange on a large plate. Scald and skin tomatoes, cut in thick slices and dust with sugar.

Soak the gelatine in the tomato juice, dissolve over gentle heat and add to the mayonnaise. When the mayonnaise begins to thicken coat the eggs, using a large tablespoon,

1 Pounding cod's roe, butter and sieved yolks together in a mortar
2 Filling mixture into egg whites
3 Sandwiching filled halves of egg
4 Finished eggs à la grecque

Anchovy eggs

and let mayonnaise run from the bowl of the spoon. Arrange the eggs on a serving dish. Mix together a dressing of oil, seasonings and lemon juice and pour on to tomatoes; arrange these with eggs on serving dish. Cut the lemon rind in fine shreds and cook in boiling water for 1 minute. Drain, dry on absorbent paper and scatter over the tomato salad.

4 eggs (hard-boiled)
6-12 anchovy fillets (soaked in 2 tablespoons milk)
2 oz butter
black pepper (ground from mill)
½ pint thick mayonnaise (page 137)
1 dessertspoon freshly chopped mixed herbs — optional
watercress (to garnish)

This is a good dish for a first course.

Method
Hardboil the eggs, quickly cool them, peel and then cut in half lengthways. Soak the anchovies in milk to remove the excess salt, then drain them, unless they have soaked up all the milk, and pound until smooth. Work butter and egg yolks into anchovies. Season with black pepper.

Fill the egg whites with the anchovy mixture and sandwich the halves together again.

Serve the eggs coated with mayonnaise, lightly flavoured with the herbs. Garnish with sprays of watercress.

4

Oeufs au cresson

(Egg and watercress mayonnaise)

4-5 eggs (hard-boiled)
1 oz butter
¼ pint thick mayonnaise (page 137)
salt and pepper
2 bunches of watercress
squeeze of lemon
pinch of cayenne pepper, or 2-3 drops of Tabasco sauce
1-2 tablespoons French dressing (see page 136)
extra watercress (to garnish) — optional

Method

Cut the eggs in half lengthways, remove the yolks and rub them through a wire strainer. Soften the butter, work in the egg yolks and about 1 teaspoon of thick mayonnaise, season well. Cover the yolk mixture and keep the egg whites in a bowl of cold water.

Boil 1 bunch of watercress for 5 minutes, then drain it well and sieve. Add watercress purée to the mayonnaise with a squeeze of lemon and cayenne (or Tabasco sauce). Chop the second bunch of watercress coarsely and mix with the French dressing and place in the serving dish.

Dry the egg whites, fill with creamed yolk mixture and reshape eggs. Arrange them on the chopped watercress and coat with the mayonnaise. Garnish with slices of lemon and a spray of watercress if wished. Serve with brown bread and butter.

The watercress purée is mixed into the mayonnaise before adding a squeeze of lemon juice, and a little cayenne pepper or Tabasco sauce

Placing the eggs filled with creamed yolk mixture on a bed of chopped watercress and French dressing, for coating with mayonnaise

Oeufs au cresson arranged on chopped watercress mixed with French dressing and garnished with lemon and a spray of watercress

Pipérade

5 eggs
$\frac{3}{4}$ lb ripe tomatoes
2 sweet red peppers, or 2-3 caps of canned pimiento
2 oz butter
1 shallot (finely chopped)
2 cloves of garlic (finely chopped)
salt and pepper
little garlic butter (see page 142)

This Basque dish of peppers eggs and tomatoes is flavoured with garlic ; it can be eaten cold or hot.

Method
Scald and skin the tomatoes, squeeze to remove seeds and chop flesh roughly. Remove the seeds from peppers and chop, blanch and drain (or drain and chop pimiento).

Melt half the butter in a deep frying pan ; put in the tomatoes, peppers, shallot and garlic. Season well, cook slowly, stirring occasionally, until it is a rich pulp.

Break eggs into a bowl and beat up with a fork. Add remaining butter and eggs to pan and stir with a metal spoon until they start to thicken creamily. Turn on to a dish and leave to cool. Cut in wedges and serve with salad.

For a picnic, cut off the top (lid) of a small French loaf and scoop out most of the crumb. Spread inside and out with garlic butter, including the top. Bake in oven at 350°F or Mark 4 until slightly crisp. Fill with pipérade, replace lid ; when cold, slice loaf.

To serve hot : make pipérade as above, turn into hot serving dish and surround with croûtes, both sides of which are spread with garlic butter.

Eggs dijonnaise

6 eggs (hard-boiled)
2 oz Cheshire cheese (finely grated)

For mayonnaise
2-3 egg yolks
salt and pepper
1 teaspoon French mustard
$\frac{1}{2}$ pint olive oil
2 tablespoons wine vinegar

For mushroom salad
$\frac{1}{2}$ lb firm mushrooms
3 tablespoons olive oil
1 shallot (finely chopped)
1 tablespoon red wine vinegar
salt and pepper
1 tablespoon parsley (chopped)

Method
Make the mayonnaise (see method, page 137).

Cut the eggs in half lengthways, remove the yolks and rub through a wire strainer into a bowl ; keep the whites in a bowl of cold water. Mix the yolks with the cheese and a tablespoon of mayonnaise and beat until smooth and creamy. Season to taste.

To prepare the salad : trim the stalks and wash mushrooms quickly in salted water, drain well and cut in thick slices. Heat the oil in a sauté pan, add the mushrooms and shallot and cook briskly for 1 minute only, then pour into a bowl. Add the parsley, vinegar and seasoning and leave to cool.

Dry the halved egg whites on a cloth or absorbent paper and fill them with the cheese mixture ; arrange on a serving dish. Spoon over the mustard mayonnaise and garnish with the mushroom salad.

Right : mayonnaise is at the thick stage and the rest of the oil is slowly being added ; alongside are the egg and cheese mixture, the mushroom salad and egg whites

The eggs dijonnaise arranged on a serving dish with mushroom salad

Eggs mimosa

4 large eggs (hard-boiled)
4-6 oz shrimps, or prawns
  (shelled and coarsely chopped)
$\frac{1}{2}$ pint thick mayonnaise (page 137)
watercress (to garnish)

One of the best and simplest egg dishes for a first course. Serve with·thin slices of brown bread and butter.

Method
Cool eggs and peel. Split them in half lengthways, scoop out yolks and carefully push half of them through a bowl strainer into a basin. Add the shrimps or prawns. Mix and bind with 1-2 tablespoons mayonnaise.

Wash whites, dry and set on a serving dish. Fill with the prawn mixture. Thin the rest of the mayonnaise slightly with 1 tablespoon hot water and coat the eggs with this.

Hold strainer over eggs and push rest of the yolks through. Garnish dish with watercress.

1 Sieving the egg yolks, ready to mix with the shrimps or prawns
2 Binding the mixture together with thick mayonnaise
3 Sieved egg yolks are scattered on top of the filled eggs
4 The finished dish is garnished with watercress

Eggs indochine

8 eggs (hard-boiled)
4 oz butter (well creamed)
1 teaspoon tomato purée

For salad
1 cucumber
1 teaspoon salt
1 tablespoon olive oil
$\frac{1}{2}$ teaspoon caster sugar
pepper (ground from mill)
1 teaspoon white wine vinegar
$\frac{1}{2}$ lb prawns (shelled)
1 teaspoon chopped parsley, or mint

For curry cream dressing
1 tablespoon chopped onion
1 clove of garlic (chopped)
2 tablespoons oil
1 dessertspoon curry powder
$\frac{1}{4}$ pint tomato juice
1 slice of lemon
1 tablespoon apricot jam
$\frac{1}{2}$ pint mayonnaise (see page 137)
extra lemon juice (for mayonnaise)
— optional
extra salt and pepper (for
mayonnaise) — optional

This quantity serves 6-8 people.

Method
First prepare the curry cream dressing: cook the onion and garlic in the oil until soft but not coloured, add the curry powder and continue cooking for 1 minute. Pour on the tomato juice, add the lemon and cook gently for 7-10 minutes. Stir in the apricot jam and boil up well. Strain dressing and leave to cool.

To prepare the salad: cut the cucumber into julienne strips (about $\frac{1}{8}$ inch by $1\frac{1}{2}$ -2 inches long), sprinkle with the salt, cover and leave in a cool place for about 30 minutes. Drain away liquid and wipe away any visible salt with absorbent paper. Turn cucumber gently in the oil until completely covered. Season with sugar and pepper, sprinkle on the vinegar and mix again. Mix the prawns and parsley (or mint) with the cucumber.

Halve the eggs lengthways, take out the yolks and rub them through a wire strainer; mix these with the butter, tomato purée and about 1 teaspoon of the curry mixture. Wash and dry the egg whites, fill with the mixture, and reshape. Dish up the eggs in a circle on a serving dish. Add the remaining curry dressing to the mayonnaise with extra seasoning and lemon juice added, if necessary. Use about half this sauce to coat the eggs.

Pile the salad in the centre of the dish. Serve the remaining sauce in a bowl or sauce boat.

Eggs Richelieu

6 eggs (new-laid)
1¾ pints aspic jelly made with chicken, or veal, stock (to decorate) — see page 136
1 truffle (sliced), or 1 prawn (split) — to decorate
1 bunch of watercress (optional)

For prawn mousse
about 10 oz shelled shrimps, or prawns (thaw frozen ones in the refrigerator overnight)
2½ oz unsalted butter (creamed)
¼ pint béchamel sauce (made with ¾ oz butter ¾ oz plain flour and ¼ pint flavoured milk — see method, page 136)
salt and pepper
2 tablespoons double, or single, cream

For chaudfroid sauce
¾ pint béchamel sauce (made with 1 oz butter, 1 oz plain flour and ¾ pint flavoured milk — see method, page 136)
2 tablespoons double cream
¼ oz gelatine (dissolved in 3½-4 oz of the aspic jelly)

These are French poached eggs set on a shrimp or prawn mousse, coated with a white chaudfroid, decorated with prawn or truffle and garnished with aspic. This dish is suitable for a first course for a formal or buffet luncheon.

Method
Poach the eggs in the French way, until firm to the touch, taking care to keep them plump and of good shape. Slip eggs into cold water as soon as they are cooked and leave until wanted.
To prepare the prawn mousse : dry the prawns (or shrimps) lightly with absorbent paper and put them twice through a mincer. Turn them into a mortar and pound well, gradually adding the creamed butter.

Watchpoint Do not work the prawn mousse in a blender (instead of pounding it) as this is inclined to make it rather stringy and tough, not light and smooth as it should be.
Then add 3-4 tablespoons béchamel sauce, season carefully and fold in the cream. The mousse should be light in consistency and should drop from the spoon. Chill slightly.
To prepare the chaudfroid : have ready the cooled béchamel sauce and stir in the cream and aspic in which the gelatine has been dissolved. Put through a tammy strainer into a thin saucepan. Lift the eggs out with a draining spoon and lay them on a cloth. Pat dry and turn them carefully on to a wire rack.
Set the saucepan of chaudfroid in a bowl of cold water with a few lumps of ice in it. Stir until the sauce reaches coating consistency, then spoon it over the eggs and leave to set. Coat once more and again leave to set. Decorate with the sliced truffle or split prawn, then coat with clear aspic on the point of setting. Leave for 1-2 hours.
To dish up : choose an oval silver, or steel, dish. Run a little cool aspic over the bottom and when set spoon the mousse down the centre. Smooth a little, then lift the eggs carefully with a slice and arrange them on the mousse. Have ready some set aspic, chop it and garnish the sides of the dish with this. A little watercress could also be used, if wished.

Boiled eggs in soy sauce

5 eggs
4 tablespoons soy sauce
1 teaspoon granulated sugar
1 teaspoon oil
4 tablespoons water

These eggs are good as an hors d'oeuvre.

Method
Boil the eggs for 5 minutes, cool, and remove shells. Heat all the rest of the ingredients and simmer the eggs in this liquid for 7 minutes. Draw aside and leave to steep for 30 minutes, turning the eggs occasionally to colour evenly. Drain the eggs, cut in quarters and serve cold.

Sardine and egg savoury

1 small can (4¼ oz) sardines
4 eggs (hard-boiled)
salt and pepper
2-3 drops of vinegar, or lemon juice
2 tomatoes (halved)
4 dessertspoons salad cream

Method
Split each sardine, remove the centre bone and tail and mash flesh with a fork. Halve the eggs lengthways, scoop out the yolks, add them to the sardines and mix well together until smooth. Season, and add the vinegar (or lemon juice).

Fill the egg whites with this mixture, reshape the eggs and set each one on a tomato half. Coat with salad cream and serve with brown bread and butter.

Eggs Maryland

6 eggs
4 thin slices of ham (cooked)
12 oz sweetcorn kernels (frozen, or canned)
1 cap of canned pimiento
3 tablespoons double cream (lightly whipped)
salt and pepper
paprika pepper
lemon juice
½ pint aspic jelly (cool, but still liquid) — see page 136
small cress (for garnish)

Method
Poach the eggs and keep in a bowl of cold water until wanted. Shred the ham. Drain the canned sweetcorn or cook frozen corn until tender. Shred the pimiento.

Stir the sweetcorn and pimiento into the cream. Season well with salt, pepper, paprika and lemon juice and spoon into an entrée dish. Drain and dry the eggs and place them on top of the sweetcorn mixture. Add the ham to the aspic in a bowl, stand this in a pan of ice-cold water and, when on the point of setting, spoon it over the eggs. Garnish the dish with the cress.

1 *After poaching the eggs, keep them in a bowl of cold water while preparing the other ingredients. Here the ham is being shredded into julienne strips*
2 *Mix the sweetcorn and pimiento with cream and seasoning and spoon on to entrée dish. Then drain eggs on a towel and place on top*
3 *Eggs Maryland ready to serve*

Eggs d'or

12 eggs (hard-boiled)
$\frac{1}{4}$ pint thick mayonnaise (page 137)
2-3 tablespoons sweet chutney,
  or pickle
24 small rounds of buttered
  brown bread
watercress

For sauce
2-3 tablespoons tomato juice,
  or tomato cocktail
1 teaspoon curry paste
$\frac{1}{2}$ pint mayonnaise (see page 137)
2-3 tablespoons mango chutney
2 tablespoons double cream

This quantity serves 6 people.

Method
Cut the eggs in two lengthways, scoop out the yolks and put the whites into cold water. Mix the $\frac{1}{4}$ pint thick mayonnaise with the sweet chutney (or pickle). Dry the egg whites and set them on rounds of brown bread and place in a serving dish, or serve bread separately.

Place a little of the mayonnaise mixture into the hollow of each egg white. Put the yolks into a wire sieve and press them through on to whites in a mound. Garnish with watercress.

Combine the ingredients for the sauce; first mix the tomato juice with the curry paste before adding it to the mayonnaise, then finish with the mango chutney and the cream. Serve in a sauceboat.

Watchpoint It is better not to dish up these eggs more than 30 minutes before serving otherwise the yolks will go dry. Yolks can be kept in a covered basin until you are ready to complete dishing up.

Scotch eggs

8 new-laid eggs (hard-boiled)
1 lb pork sausage meat
1 tablespoon chopped mixed herbs
salt and pepper
seasoned plain flour
1 egg (beaten)
dried white breadcrumbs (for frying)
deep fat (for frying)

Method
Mix the sausage meat with the herbs and seasoning. Have the eggs ready peeled and dried. Divide the sausage meat into equal portions. Pat these out into rounds on a dampened board, place an egg on each one and fold the sausage meat up around the egg to envelop it completely. Roll eggs in seasoned flour, brush with beaten egg and coat well with the crumbs.

Fry the Scotch eggs in deep fat until a russet-brown. Cool them before cutting in half to serve.

1 *Moulding the seasoned sausage meat round hard-boiled eggs*
2 *Frying Scotch eggs in deep fat*
3 *Scotch eggs halved, ready to serve*

Eggs à la basque

8 eggs (hard-boiled)
4 large tomatoes (skinned)
6 caps of pimiento

For dressing
1 teaspoon paprika pepper
1 teaspoon tomato purée
½ clove of garlic (crushed with
  ¼ teaspoon salt and pepper
  from the mill)
2 tablespoons red wine vinegar
5 tablespoons salad oil
little granulated sugar (optional)
2 tablespoons double cream

Method

Slice the hard-boiled eggs and cut the tomatoes in thin rounds. Shred the pimientos, keeping 2 shredded ones for garnish.

To make dressing: mix the paprika and tomato purée together, add the crushed garlic and mix to a paste. Add vinegar, then whisk in the oil and taste for seasoning. Add a little extra sugar if necessary (ie. if the vinegar is on the sharp side).

Place the eggs, tomatoes and pimiento in layers in a serving dish with two-thirds of the dressing. Finish with a layer of egg slices. Add the cream to the remaining dressing and spoon over top of the dish. Then cover the surface with a lattice of the reserved pimiento shreds.

Serve with a dish of small cheese crackers or breadsticks.

Left : layering ingredients for eggs à la basque before adding dressing
Below : the dish is finished with a lattice of shredded pimiento

Egg and beetroot salad

6 eggs (hard-boiled)
4 small, round cooked beetroot, or
  1 lb jar of pickled baby beetroot
$\frac{1}{2}$ lb small new potatoes
3 spring onions
2 teaspoons caster sugar
1 teaspoon dry mustard
$\frac{1}{4}$ teaspoon salt
black pepper (ground from mill)
1 tablespoon wine vinegar
1 tablespoon grated horseradish
3 tablespoons double cream
$\frac{1}{4}$ pint mayonnaise (see page 137)

Method

Peel and slice the beetroot, scrape and cook the potatoes and chop the spring onions. Mix the sugar, mustard, salt and pepper with the vinegar, then stir in the horseradish and the cream.

If the potatoes are very small, leave them whole; otherwise quarter or slice them, mix while still warm with the horseradish cream and the chopped onion. Mix in the sliced beetroot and turn on to a serving dish; arrange the halved eggs on top and coat with the mayonnaise.

Mixing beetroot with potatoes, horseradish cream and onions

Egg and beetroot salad arranged on a serving dish

Stuffed egg salad

18 eggs (hard-boiled)
8 oz butter
4 oz flat mushrooms
6 oz cooked chicken (free from
　skin and bone)
8 oz tunny fish (canned and flaked)
8 oz cream cheese
salt and pepper

For white sauce
1½ oz butter
3 tablespoons plain flour
¾ pint milk
salt and pepper

For rice salad
1 lb long grain rice
1 lb tomatoes
1 head of celery
1 cucumber
salt
2 green peppers
2 red peppers
1 cup of carrot (diced and
　cooked)

For French dressing
little garlic (crushed)
3 tablespoons wine vinegar
¼ pint olive oil, or groundnut oil
salt
black pepper (ground from mill)
½ teaspoon French mustard
　(optional)

To garnish
1 cap of pimiento (canned) —
　for chicken
6 black olives (for tunny fish)
4 gherkins (for cream cheese)
1 lb tomatoes
2 bunches of watercress

This salad is good for a buffet.
The quantities given will serve
12 people.

Vegetables for stuffed egg salad

Method

Cut the eggs in half lengthways;
remove the yolks, rub them
through a wire strainer and mix
with the well-creamed butter
(keep back ½ oz butter for
mushrooms). Keep the egg
whites in a bowl of cold water.

Chop the mushrooms very
finely and cook quickly in ½ oz
butter until all the moisture
is driven off; then turn out and
cool. Pass the chicken meat
through mincer twice.

Make the white sauce (see
page 141). Set aside to cool.

Divide egg yolk and butter
mixture into three; mix one
portion with the chicken and
mushrooms, a second with the
flaked tunny fish and the third
with the cream cheese. Add
enough cold white sauce to each
mixture to bind, and season to
taste.

To prepare the rice salad: cook the rice in plenty of boiling, salted water until tender — about 12 minutes. Tip rice into a colander, rinse in hot water to remove starch and drain well. Turn on to a large, flat dish to dry.

Scald and skin 1 lb tomatoes (see page 141), cut into four and take out seeds; then cut the quarters into large strips. Wash celery and slice; dice cucumber, sprinkle with salt, lay on a plate, cover and leave 20-30 minutes to draw out excess water. Cut peppers in half, remove core and seeds, then cut in shreds; blanch in boiling water, cook 1 minute, drain and refresh in cold water.

Next make the French dressing (see page 136); season well with a little garlic crushed in a bowl with the salt, black pepper and French mustard.

Drain liquid from the cucumber, dry in absorbent paper. Use a fork to mix all the vegetables and rice together, taste for seasoning, then bind with French dressing. Spoon salad on to three large dishes.

Drain and dry egg whites and place firmly on rice. Fill egg whites with the different mixtures (or pipe in fillings using an 8-cut vegetable rose nozzle for the cream cheese, and a $\frac{1}{2}$-inch éclair nozzle for the other two mixtures).

To garnish: decorate chicken mixture with a 'diamond' of pimiento, the tunny fish with half a black olive, and cream cheese with a good slice of gherkin. Fill middle of each dish with a large bouquet of watercress and arrange remaining tomatoes (skinned and quartered) around dishes, one between each egg.

A stuffed egg salad makes an attractive and substantial buffet lunch

Leek and egg salad

4-5 leeks (according to size)
salt
little French dressing (see page 136)
3 eggs (hard-boiled)
¼- ½ pint mayonnaise (see page 137)
paprika pepper

Method

Wash the leeks thoroughly. Split in half lengthways and tie together to form a neat bundle. Boil in salted water until just tender (about 12 minutes), drain and refresh. Untie, put in dish and pour over a little French dressing.

Cut white of eggs into strips and scatter over the leeks. Sieve yolks through a wire bowl strainer. Thin the mayonnaise, if necessary, with 1 tablespoon of boiling water. Spoon this over the salad to coat leeks, and sprinkle sieved yolks on top. Dust with paprika pepper and serve lightly chilled.

Spiced ham and egg salad

12 eggs (hard-boiled)
1 lb sliced ham
1 teaspoon paprika pepper
salt and pepper
dash of Tabasco sauce
2 tablespoons red wine vinegar
4 tablespoons tomato ketchup
6 tablespoons salad oil
3 tablespoons mango chutney
1 pinch of saffron (soaked in 2 tablespoons boiling water for about 30 minutes)
½ pint mayonnaise (see page 137)
1 lb long grain rice (boiled, drained and dried well)
watercress (to garnish)

Method

Mix the paprika, salt and pepper and Tabasco with the vinegar and stir in the tomato ketchup. Then add the oil, whisk well until the mixture thickens and taste for seasoning. If the mango chutney is rather coarse, cut the mango into thin strips ; add to the dressing. Cut the ham into shreds and mix with the dressing.

Strain the saffron liquid through a nylon strainer and beat into the mayonnaise. Taste the mayonnaise for seasoning and then mix into the rice. Arrange this rice on a serving dish. Cut the hard-boiled eggs in half and arrange on top of the rice. Spoon the spiced ham mixture over the eggs and garnish the dish with watercress.

Tunny fish and egg salad

2 cans (7½ oz each) tunny fish
4 eggs (hard-boiled)
2 lb tomatoes
1½ cucumbers (peeled)
salt
1 lb frozen French, or sliced,
  beans
1 small can anchovy fillets
1 tablespoon mixed chopped
  herbs (½ parsley, ¼ mint and
  ¼ chives)
French dressing (made from
  2 tablespoons white wine
  vinegar, salt and pepper,
  6 tablespoons salad oil — see
  method, page 136)
12 black olives (halved and stoned)

Large gratin dish

If no fresh herbs are available,
use ½ tablespoon dried basil
and oregano (mixed).

Method

Scald and skin the tomatoes;
cut ½ lb into quarters and the
remainder in thick slices. Slice
the half cucumber very finely,
salt it and keep between 2
plates. Cut the other cucumber
in thicker slices, or into small
cubes, and sprinkle with salt.
Cook the beans in boiling water
until tender and then drain and
refresh. Drain the anchovy fillets
from the oil and cut each fillet
in half lengthways.

Flake the tunny fish and slice
the hard-boiled eggs. Layer the
sliced tomatoes, beans and
thickly cut cucumber (drained
of the water), tunny fish and
hard-boiled eggs in a large
gratin dish. Add the herbs to
the French dressing, whisk well
and spoon over the salad.
Place the thinly cut cucumber,
also drained of water, over the
top of the salad. Arrange the
anchovy fillets in a lattice over
the top of the cucumber and
place a half olive in each
square. Arrange the quartered
tomatoes around the outside
of the dish.

Serve with potatoes baked
in their jackets.

Decorating Easter eggs

If you want to give the children a simple treat, boil their breakfast eggs in water with a few drops of different edible colourings.

To make animals or nursery rhyme characters, cut hats, long ears or silhouettes from felt, stick them on with strong adhesive; or make up your own designs with water paints (the non-toxic kind).

For very special eggs (see right) to be eaten cold, hard-boiled, or for use as table decoration, you need more ingenuity.

Select smooth-shelled white eggs. Collect primroses, primulas and, if possible, pieces of fern, which should be blanched for 1 minute in boiling water to soften them enough to adhere to the eggs.

For yellow and orange colourings use onion skins; for soft purple, fawn and grey colourings, use birch bark; red primulas give a bluish-green pattern. First pluck the flower from its stem, then wet an egg and place flowers on it to form a pattern. Hold flowers in position, cover with onion skins or birch bark, and while holding firmly, bandage tightly with 1-inch strips cut from any suitable cloth or bandage. Keep all in place with two elastic bands.

Put the egg into a pan of cold water and bring it gently to the boil, then simmer for about 15 minutes. Cool in cold water and peel off the bandage strips. The dyed eggs may then be washed before serving.

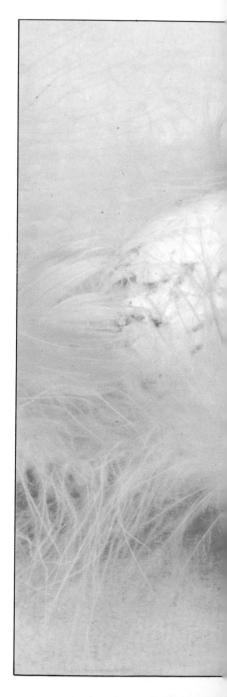

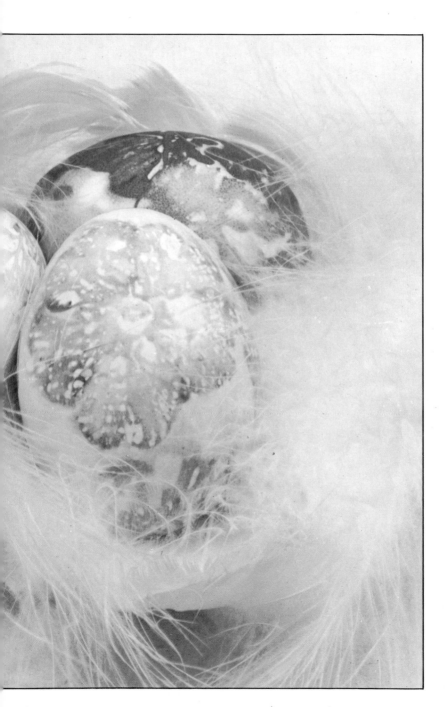

Eggs à l'estragon

(with tarragon)

4-5 small eggs (new-laid)
about 1½ pints chicken aspic (see page 136)
tarragon leaves (to garnish)
3-4 oz ham (thinly sliced) — optional

4-5 individual cocottes

A simple and delicious dish for a summer's day. Make it with chicken aspic that is not too firmly set.

Method

Poach the eggs and put them into cold water until wanted. Have ready the aspic, liquid but cool, and the cocottes. Dip the tarragon leaves (or small sprigs) into boiling water for a second.

Drain eggs carefully and dry well on absorbent paper. Trim them, if necessary, and place each one in a cocotte.

Pour a little aspic into a small saucepan or enamel measure (which cools quickly) ; stand this in iced water or on ice. Stir aspic gently with a metal spoon until just cold but not set, then spoon enough into each cocotte to cover the egg. Arrange 2-3 leaves of the tarragon on top and leave cocottes until aspic is set. Then fill to the brim with remaining aspic which should be on the point of setting. Put in the refrigerator or in a cold place until set.

Optional addition : first shred the ham ; divide this between the cocottes, add a little cold aspic and leave until just set before putting in the eggs. Finish as above.

Eggs en gelée

(eggs in aspic)

4-5 small eggs (new-laid)
2 pints chicken aspic (cool but liquid) — see page 136
4-5 slices of ham (wafer-thin)
1 small lettuce, or chopped aspic (to garnish)

4-5 oval dariole moulds (about 2½ inches deep)

These are soft-boiled eggs (eggs mollets) rolled in slices of ham and set in individual moulds.

Method

Softboil the eggs, peel carefully and keep in cold water until wanted. Have ready the aspic, pour enough into each mould to cover the bottom by a good ¼ inch ; leave to set.

Drain eggs and dry them thoroughly, wrap each one in a slice of ham and put into a mould. Fill to the brim with cool aspic, then leave it to set.

Turn out eggs, arrange them in a serving dish, garnish with lettuce leaves or chopped aspic. **Watchpoint** The eggs must be small (from pullets) so that once in the moulds they do not rise over the edge. Otherwise they will not sit flat when turned out.

More desserts made with eggs

Smooth delicious custards and creams, light fluffy soufflés and rich sweet soufflé omelets — all our favourite desserts are made with eggs.

Custards particularly play an important part in cooking, they form the base of many, many sweets or make delicious sauces for cooked fruit and hot puddings. There are two types of custard. The first is when eggs and milk are mixed together and baked, or steamed, to set firm. The second is when egg yolks and milk are cooked over a gentle heat to a creamy consistency. This is the soft custard that forms the basis of cream desserts and soufflés.

Remember that egg whites set a custard and the yolks give it its creamy consistency. For a baked or steamed custard you need 2 whole eggs and 2 egg yolks to 1 pint of milk. For a custard base, take 4 yolks to a pint of milk, but whites tend to curdle the mixture.

Any mixture of egg and milk will curdle if allowed to get too hot, so for baking a custard in the oven it is wise to use a bain-marie. For a soft custard, scald the milk by bringing it up to boiling point. You can use a double saucepan with hot water in the lower pan, or, with care, the custard can be thickened on direct, but gentle, heat.

Soufflés are based on a custard mixture, but they benefit by the addition of 1 extra white to yolks. Though this is not essential it makes for a lighter, fluffier mixture.

Caramel cream (Crème caramel)

1 pint milk
2 eggs
2 egg yolks
1½ tablespoons caster sugar

For caramel
4 oz lump, or granulated, sugar
½ cup water

*6-inch diameter (size No. 2) soufflé
dish, or 6-inch diameter cake tin*

Method

Scald milk. Break eggs into a bowl, then add the extra yolks. Beat well with a fork but do not allow to get frothy. Add sugar and milk, mix and set aside until needed.

Set oven at 375°F or Mark 5.

Put sugar and water for caramel into a small pan, dissolve sugar over a gentle heat, then boil rapidly without stirring until a rich brown in colour. Stop boiling by dipping bottom of pan into a basin of cold water and, when still, pour three-quarters of caramel into a dry and warm soufflé dish or cake tin; pour rest on to an oiled plate or tin. Turn soufflé dish or cake tin carefully round to coat the caramel evenly over the bottom and sides.

Strain in the custard mixture, cover with foil or a piece of buttered paper. Cook in a bain-marie in the pre-set oven for 40-50 minutes until just set; take out and leave until cool before turning out. Crush the rest of the caramel and put round the dish.

Watchpoint A certain amount of caramel will always be left in the mould after turning out; this can be lessened by adding 1 teaspoon boiling water to caramel before pouring it into soufflé dish or cake tin. For a more creamy-textured custard use an extra egg yolk.

Coat caramel round sides of the dish, then strain in the custard

Petits pots de crème (Small pots of cream)

1½ pints milk
vanilla pod
3 eggs
3 egg yolks
1 tablespoon vanilla sugar
2 tablespoons caster sugar
2 teaspoons instant coffee
2 oz plain block chocolate
(broken up)

Deep mousse pots, or ramekins

Made in a variety of flavours and arranged on a large dish, these 'petits pots' look good on a buffet table.

Method

Warm all the milk with the vanilla pod, remove from heat and leave to infuse 5-10 minutes until well flavoured. Meanwhile, break 1 of the eggs into a bowl, add 1 yolk and 1 tablespoon vanilla sugar, and beat well a fork, but do not allow to get frothy. Remove the vanilla pod from milk, and pour ½ pint on to eggs and sugar. Blend well, strain and pour into pots.

Using the same bowl, beat 1 egg, 1 egg yolk and 1 tablespoon caster sugar. Warm the remaining milk slightly, and pour ½ pint of it on to eggs and sugar. Blend in the coffee, making sure it has thoroughly dissolved, strain and pour into pots.

Again using the same bowl (any leftover coffee will improve the flavour of the chocolate), beat the remaining egg, egg yolk and sugar. Simmer the chocolate in remaining ½ pint milk for 2-3 minutes. Pour on to the eggs and sugar, blend, strain and pour into pots.

Place the filled pots in water in a bain-marie, or in a deep ovenproof dish on a baking

sheet, covered with buttered paper. Cook in oven pre-set at 350-375°F or Mark 4-5 for 12-15 minutes until just set. Take out and chill. Serve plain or with cream.

Custard pudding

1 pint milk
strip of lemon rind (optional)
2 eggs
2 egg yolks
1 ½ tablespoons caster sugar
2-3 drops of vanilla essence
    (optional)
butter
nutmeg (grated) — optional

7-inch diameter pie dish

Method
Set oven at 350-375°F or Mark 4-5.

Butter the pie dish. Scald the milk (with the lemon rind). Beat the eggs and yolks together until well mixed but not frothy. Add the sugar (and the vanilla). Pour on the milk, blend, take out the lemon rind if being used and strain custard into the pie dish. Dot the surface with a little butter and grate over a little nutmeg if wished.

Stand the dish in a bain-marie and cook in the pre-set oven for 35-40 minutes. The pudding should be just set and have a nice brown top. Serve hot or cold.

Tangerine cream

3 tangerines, or clementines
6-8 sugar lumps
¾ pint milk
1 tablespoon caster sugar
3 egg yolks
¾ oz gelatine
5 tablespoons cold water
1 egg white
¼ pint double cream
2-3 tablespoons redcurrant jelly

Glass dessert bowl

Method
Rub the sugar lumps over the rind of the washed tangerines or clementines to remove all the zest. When well soaked with the zest, put sugar lumps in a pan with the milk and dissolve over a gentle heat. Beat yolks well with caster sugar in a bowl. Pour on the milk, return to the pan and stir over the heat until it thickens ; do not let milk boil. Strain and cool.

Soften the gelatine in the water in a small pan, then heat until dissolved. Whip the egg white and then the cream. Mix the two together. Add gelatine to custard : when beginning to thicken, fold in cream mixture. Turn into bowl to set.

Meanwhile peel and slice the tangerines or clementines. Dissolve the redcurrant jelly over a gentle heat with about 3 tablespoons of water to make a syrup. Strain or beat it until smooth. Leave until cold. Arrange the slices of tangerine or clementines over the cream ; before serving, coat with syrup.

Bavarian cream (Bavarois à la crème)

3 egg yolks
2 tablespoons caster sugar
1 vanilla pod, or 2-3 drops of
  vanilla essence
$\frac{3}{4}$ pint milk
$\frac{3}{4}$ oz gelatine
5 tablespoons water
$\frac{1}{4}$ pint double cream

Plain mould (1½ pints capacity)

Method

Cream yolks thoroughly with sugar in a bowl. Infuse pod in milk until well flavoured, or add vanilla essence to the yolk mixture. Pour milk on to the yolks, first taking out the vanilla pod. Blend well and return to the pan. Stir continually over the heat until the custard coats back of the spoon. Strain into bowl to cool.

Put the gelatine into a small pan, add the water, leave to soak for 4-5 minutes. Partially whip the cream. When the custard is cold, dissolve the gelatine over the heat. It should be quite hot before pouring into the custard. Turn into a thin pan and stand in a bowl of cold water (for quickness add a little ice to the water). Stir until beginning to thicken creamily, then add 2 tablespoons of the partially whipped cream.

Turn custard into a lightly oiled mould, leave to set. Then turn out carefully and spread over the rest of the cream. If wished, additional cream can be used for decorating. In this case use the whole $\frac{1}{4}$ pint for the mixture.

For a coffee bavarois : add 1 tablespoon instant coffee to the milk while bringing it to scalding point, then pour on to the yolks.

For a chocolate bavarois : break up 4 oz plain dessert chocolate and cook for 3-4 minutes in the milk.

For a good party sweet for 6-8 people, make two lots of bavarois, say a vanilla and a chocolate one. Pour the vanilla into a large plain cake tin and, when just about to set, pour in the chocolate. Gently stir round once or twice to marble the colours. Leave to set, turn out and edge with cream (or pipe a ruff of cream) round the base.

Bavarois is the name given to a rich egg custard stiffened or set with gelatine, and whipped cream added before turning into a mould. It should be velvety in consistency and must only just hold its shape when turned out.

All custard-based desserts set with gelatine should be eaten the day they are made as the consistency tends to toughen if kept for any length of time.

Coupe française

¼ pint milk
thinly pared rind of ½ lemon
2 egg yolks
1 oz caster sugar
1 teaspoon gelatine (soaked in 2
   tablespoons water) — see
   page 137
½ teaspoon vanilla essence
1 small carton (2½ fl oz) double
   cream
1 egg white

To finish
bright red canned cherries, or about
   20 fresh strawberries with 1
   tablespoon caster sugar

4-5 coupe glasses

Method

Infuse the milk with the lemon rind. Cream the egg yolks and sugar together until thick and light in colour. Remove lemon rind and tip the hot milk on to the yolks then strain back into the saucepan.

Stir the mixture over gentle heat until the custard coats the back of the wooden spoon, then add the soaked gelatine and stir until melted.

Watchpoint Do not allow to boil. To cut down the risk of over-heating and consequent curdling, a double saucepan, or a bowl over a pan of hot water, may be used to thicken the custard.

Cool the mixture, then add the vanilla essence and cream. Whisk the egg white until stiff, fold into the creamy mixture with a metal spoon and stir gently (standing the bowl in a second one containing ice cubes and water) until the mixture begins to thicken. Pour quickly into the coupe glasses and leave until set.

Arrange the drained cherries or the strawberries (sprinkled

with sugar), in a pyramid on top **3**
of each coupe.

Serve as cold as possible.

1 *Tipping the infused milk, while
still hot, on to thickly creamed egg
yolks and sugar*

2 *Testing the custard for coating
consistency before adding gelatine*

3 *Folding stiffly whisked egg white
into the cool custard, cream and
vanilla mixture*

4 *Coupe française, chilled for
serving, with cherries piled on top*

Peruvian cream

scant 1¼ pints milk
2¼ oz coffee beans
1-2 drops of vanilla essence
3½ oz caster sugar
2 tablespoons hot water
3¼ oz plain block chocolate
5 egg yolks
1 whole egg

*6-inch diameter top (size No. 2)
souffié dish, or shallow pie dish
(1½ pints capacity)*

Method
Infuse the milk with the coffee beans; when well flavoured, strain it and add the vanilla essence. Cook the caster sugar to a light caramel in a small pan; stop further cooking by touching the base of the pan in cold water. Add the hot water to caramel and dissolve over gentle heat. Keep this on one side.

Break up the chocolate, place it in a pan with a little of the coffee-flavoured milk and dissolve it over very gentle heat. Work it until the chocolate is smooth, then add to the remaining milk with the caramel. Beat yolks and egg, pour on the liquid, then turn cream into the dish; cook gently au ,bain-marie for about 25 minutes until set. Remove dish and leave to cool.

To serve, leave cream plain or cover with lightly whipped cream and decorate with grated chocolate.

Maple mousse

12 oz maple syrup
scant ½ oz gelatine (soaked in 3 tablespoons cold water) — see page 137
6 egg yolks
1¾ pints double cream
1-2 oz flaked, or chopped, or toasted, almonds (for decoration) — see page 138
1 tablespoon rum

This dish will serve 8.

Method
Heat the maple syrup in a double boiler and, when hot, add the soaked gelatine and stir until dissolved. Beat the egg yolks until very light, add a little of the hot syrup to them and then mix all the egg yolk into the syrup mixture.

When the syrup mixture is cool, whip the cream and fold in 1½ pints; pour into a glass bowl and put in the refrigerator to set — allow 2 hours for this. Cover the top with the almonds and serve with the remaining whipped cream flavoured with the rum.

Chocolate roulade

6 oz block chocolate
5 eggs
8 oz caster sugar
3-4 tablespoons water

For filling
½ pint double cream (lightly whipped
and flavoured with vanilla
essence, or rum, or brandy)
icing sugar (for dusting)

Shallow swiss roll tin (12 inches by 8 inches), or roulade case (see page 27)

Method

Line tin with oiled greaseproof paper, or brush the paper case with oil or melted shortening. Set the oven at 350°F or Mark 4.

Separate the eggs, beat the yolks with sugar, adding them gradually until mixture is lemon coloured. Melt chocolate in water in a pan over gentle heat and, when it is a thick cream, draw pan aside. Whip the egg whites to a firm snow, then add chocolate to egg yolks mixture ; cut and fold egg whites into the mixture and turn it into the prepared tin or case. Place in pre-set moderate oven and bake for 10-15 minutes or until firm to the touch.

Have ready a clean cloth, wrung out in cold water. Take out the roulade, cool it slightly, then cover with the cloth. (This is to prevent any sugary crust forming.) Leave it in a cool place for 12 hours or in a refrigerator overnight.

Lay a piece of greaseproof paper on a table, dust it well with icing sugar. Remove the cloth and turn the roulade upside down on to the prepared paper ; strip paper case off the roulade carefully, (or remove swiss roll tin), spread with the whipped cream and roll it up like a swiss roll. Lift on to a serving dish and dust well with icing sugar.

Note : for serving at Christmas, the cream filling can be mixed with a little dry, sieved chestnut ; otherwise serve the roulade as it is.

Charlotte mexicaine

2 oz coffee beans
1 pint milk
6 oz plain block chocolate
5 egg yolks
2 oz caster sugar
½ oz gelatine (dissolved in
    2½ fl oz water) — see page 137
7½ fl oz double cream
1 egg white

For decoration
langues de chats biscuits
¼-½ pint double cream
squares, or rounds, of chocolate
    (optional)

7-8 inch diameter cake tin

Method

Lightly oil the cake tin. Infuse coffee beans in the milk for 10-12 minutes over gentle heat; do not allow milk to boil. Cut up the block chocolate and put it into a pan, then strain on a little of the coffee-flavoured milk. Dissolve chocolate over gentle heat, then strain on the rest of the milk and blend well.

Work the egg yolks and sugar well together, pour on the milk, stir to blend and return to the pan. Stir until the custard will coat the back of the spoon but do not allow it to boil; strain and leave it to cool.

Add the gelatine liquid to the custard and turn it into a thin pan; set this in a bowl of cold water or on ice. When it is on the point of setting, partially whip the cream, whisk the egg white, add it to the cream, then fold both into the chocolate. Turn this into the prepared tin and leave to set.

Turn out the charlotte and lightly whip the remaining cream. Spread the sides of the charlotte with a little of the cream and arrange the biscuits around, overlapping them slightly, then decorate the top with the remaining cream, and the squares (or rounds) of chocolate.

Orange soufflé

3 oz lump sugar
2 oranges
½ pint milk
1 rounded tablespoon plain flour
1 oz butter
3 egg yolks
4 egg whites
little sifted icing sugar

7-inch diameter top (size No. 1) soufflé dish

Method

Prepare soufflé dish (see pages 25 and 26). Set oven at 375°F or Mark 5.

Rub some of the lumps of sugar over the outside rind of the oranges until they are soaked with the oil (zest). Then set aside.

Mix 3 tablespoons of the milk with the flour until smooth. Scald remaining milk, add all the sugar lumps and cover. Leave to infuse for 5-7 minutes off the heat. Then return pan to heat. Add the flour mixture gradually and stir until boiling. Boil 2-3 seconds, then draw aside and dot the surface with the butter. Cover and leave for 5 minutes.

Beat in egg yolks, one at a time. Whip whites to a firm snow, stir in 1 tablespoon, then cut and stir in remainder, using a metal spoon. Turn at once into prepared dish and bake in pre-set oven for about 18-20 minutes or until well risen.

Then draw out oven shelf with soufflé on it, dust top quickly with icing sugar and return shelf. Cook for a further 4-5 minutes to caramelise the top. Serve at once.

Chocolate soufflé

4 oz plain block chocolate (cut in small pieces)
2 tablespoons water
½ pint milk
2 rounded tablespoons caster sugar
2-3 drops of vanilla essence
1 tablespoon plain flour
1 dessertspoon arrowroot
1 oz butter
3 egg yolks
4 egg whites
little sifted icing sugar

7-inch diameter top (size No. 1) soufflé dish

Method

Prepare soufflé dish (see pages 25 and 26). Set oven at 375°F or Mark 5.

Cut chocolate into small pieces, put into a medium-size pan with the water and stir over slow heat until melted. Add milk, reserving 4 tablespoons. Bring milk and chocolate to the boil, add sugar and vanilla, cover pan and draw aside.

Blend reserved milk with flour and arrowroot, pour this into the chocolate, return to heat and bring to the boil, stirring all the time. Boil for 2-3 seconds, then draw aside, dot surface with small pieces of butter, cover and leave for 5 minutes. Then stir to mix in butter thoroughly and beat in yolks one at a time.

Whip whites to a firm snow, cut and stir 1 tablespoon into the mixture, using a metal spoon, then stir in the rest.

Turn mixture into the prepared soufflé dish and bake in pre-set oven for 20 minutes.

Caramelise top as for orange soufflé (left). Serve at once.

119

Soufflé chinois

¾ pint milk
3 egg yolks
2 oz caster sugar
2 tablespoons syrup (from the preserved ginger)
½ oz gelatine (soaked in 4 tablespoons cold water) — see page 137
¼ pint double cream
3 egg whites
2 tablespoons preserved ginger (sliced)

For decoration
few extra preserved ginger slices
pistachio nuts (finely chopped),
    or almonds (browned) — optional

6-inch diameter top (size No. 2) soufflé dish

The custard is turned into a large, thin pan resting on a bed of ice, which helps to cool custard more quickly. Half the cream, ginger and whisked egg whites are folded in. The mixture is stirred until it begins to thicken, when it should be turned immediately into the soufflé dish

Method
Prepare soufflé dish (see pages 25 and 26).

Scald the milk in a pan. Beat the egg yolks and sugar together until thick and light in colour, add the ginger syrup and pour on the hot milk. Return to the pan and stir over a gentle heat until the mixture thickens. Strain it into a bowl, add the soaked gelatine and stir until it is dissolved. Cover the bowl of custard to prevent a skin forming and allow to cool.

Whip the cream lightly until it begins to thicken and whisk the egg whites until stiff but not dry. Turn the custard into a large thin pan, stand this in a bowl of cold water containing 3-4 ice cubes and stir until the mixture begins to thicken (a metal saucepan cools it more quickly than a china bowl).

Then take a metal spoon and quickly fold in half the cream, the sliced ginger and the whisked egg whites. Stir very carefully, holding the pan in the ice-cold water, and as the mixture begins to thicken, turn it into the prepared soufflé dish and put in a cool place to set.

When set, peel away the paper around soufflé dish. The easiest and quickest way to do this is to dip a palette or table knife in very hot water and slip it between the two thicknesses of paper (the heat loosens them).

Whisk the remaining cream and use to coat and decorate the top of the soufflé. Sprinkle with nuts, if wanted, and arrange the extra ginger slices around the top.

Soufflé chinois — half of the cream is used to coat and decorate top, together with slices of preserved ginger. You may like to sprinkle over some chopped nuts

Soufflé Rothschild

selection of ripe fruit, eg. 1 peach,
  4 strawberries, 1 banana, 1 thin
  slice of pineapple
2 tablespoons rum, or kirsch, or
  curaçao
sifted icing sugar (for dusting)

For soufflé mixture
3 egg yolks
1 tablespoon caster sugar
1 rounded tablespoon whipped
  double cream
4 egg whites

To caramelise top
2-3 tablespoons sifted icing sugar

*6-inch diameter top (size No. 2)
  soufflé dish*

Make this hot soufflé, which is
allied to a soufflé omelet mixture,
when a good selection of fresh
fruit is available.

Method
Prepare soufflé dish (see pages
25 and 26), and set oven at
375°F or Mark 5. Slice fruit
thinly, pour over chosen liqueur
and dust with icing sugar to
taste. Cover and leave for 30
minutes.

Cream egg yolks with caster
sugar, add any liquid drained
from the fruit and the whipped
cream. Whip whites to a firm
snow, then cut and fold into
mixture, using a metal spoon.

Turn one-third of this mixture
into the soufflé dish, put half
the lightly drained fruit over
the top and cover with another
third of the mixture. Finish with
the remaining fruit and mixture.

Bake in pre-set oven for
15-20 minutes. After 12 minutes
dredge quickly with icing sugar
and continue the baking to
caramelise the top.

Soufflé omelet (oven method)

4 egg yolks
1 rounded tablespoon caster sugar
grated rind and juice of $\frac{1}{2}$ lemon
5 egg whites
$\frac{1}{2}$ oz butter
little sifted icing sugar
2-3 tablespoons warm jam, or other
  filling

Oval ovenproof dish

Method
Set oven at 375°F or Mark 5.
Well butter an ovenproof dish
and dust with icing sugar.

Work yolks with sugar and
lemon rind. Add a squeeze of
the juice. Whip whites stiffly,
then cut and fold into the
mixture, using a metal spoon.
Turn mixture into the dish and
shape into an omelet with a
palette knife by making hollow
or trough down the centre. Dust
with icing sugar.

Bake in pre-set oven for
7-10 minutes, or until lightly
coloured. Spread hollow or
trough with warm jam and
serve at once.

Jam omelet

4 large eggs (separated)
1 tablespoon caster sugar
2 tablespoons single cream, or
    creamy milk
apricot, or strawberry, or goose-
    berry jam (preferably home-made)
½ oz butter
little sifted icing sugar

*2-3 metal skewers ; 8-inch diameter
    omelet pan*

Alternative fillings are fresh sliced strawberries mixed with 1 tablespoon of warm redcurrant jelly, or 2-3 bananas sliced and sautéd in a little butter, dusted with caster sugar and sprinkled with lemon juice.

Spread warm jam over the cooked omelet with a palette knife

Method
Mix egg yolks with the sugar and cream. Warm 2-3 tablespoons of the jam in a small saucepan. Whip whites to a firm snow and cut and fold into the yolk mixture, using a metal spoon. Set oven at 400°F or Mark 6 or turn on grill. Heat omelet pan until moderately hot, and put skewers in flame or under grill until red hot.

Slide omelet on to a warm dish or plate ; flip over with knife

Drop butter into the pan and, while still foaming, put in the egg mixture. Spread out in the pan and cook on moderate heat for less than 1 minute to allow the bottom to brown. Do not stir during this time.

Then slide pan into pre-set oven or under the grill to set the top. Spread omelet quickly with jam, fold over with a palette knife ; turn or slide on to a hot dish, dredge with icing sugar and mark a lattice across the top with red-hot skewers. (Heat several skewers at a time rather than heating them one by one.)

Dredge with icing sugar ; use hot skewers to make the lattice pattern

Custard sauce

(Crème à la vanille)

½ pint creamy milk
2 tablespoons caster sugar
2-3 drops of vanilla essence, or
  ½ vanilla pod (split)
2 egg yolks

Method

Put the milk in a pan, add the sugar with vanilla essence or, if using a vanilla pod, infuse it in milk for 10 minutes, keeping pan covered. Take out pod, then add sugar.

Cream the yolks in a bowl, bring the milk to scalding point and pour on gradually. Blend mixture together and return to the pan; stir continually over a gentle heat with a wooden spatula or spoon. Stir gently to avoid splashing. When the custard coats the spoon and looks creamy, strain back into the bowl.

Dredge a little caster sugar over the top and leave to cool. This coating of sugar melts and helps prevent a skin forming.

Watchpoint Should the custard get too hot and begin to curdle, turn at once into the basin without straining and whisk briskly for 2-3 seconds. Remember that gentle heat helps to prevent a custard from curdling and makes it creamier.

Oeufs à la neige

3 egg whites
3½ oz icing sugar (sifted)
2-3 drops of vanilla essence
¾ pint milk
piece of vanilla pod
4 egg yolks
2 oz caster sugar
1 tablespoon grated chocolate

Method

Whisk the egg whites until stiff and fold in the icing sugar and vanilla essence to make meringue mixture.

Put the milk into a shallow pan (sauté pan) with the vanilla pod, and bring to the boil, then remove vanilla pod. Shape the meringues with two dessert-spoons and drop into the milk. Poach carefully until firm to the touch (about 5-8 minutes), turning gently with a fork. Drain on muslin or a paper towel.

Cream the egg yolks thoughly in a bowl with the sugar, strain on the milk used for poaching the meringues and blend. Strain custard and, when quite cold, pour it into a shallow glass bowl. Put the 'eggs' on top of the 'snow' and dust with the chocolate. Serve chilled.

Meringues

A meringue is simplicity itself. Pure egg white and sugar, it makes the simplest fruit dessert into a culinary delight, or, alone with cream, nothing could be more delicious in a 'cakes and tea' setting.

There are three distinct types of meringue, though, used for different purposes in desserts, gâteaux and pâtisseries. **Meringue suisse** is the one most frequently made. The proportion of sugar to egg white never

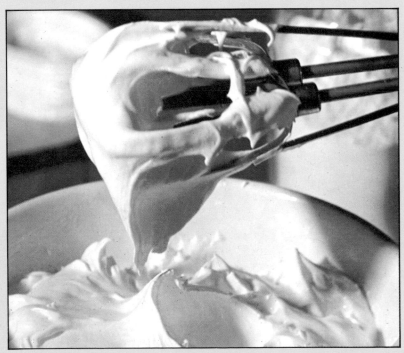

varies, being 2 oz caster sugar to each egg white, which is stiffly whipped before the sugar is folded in. This meringue is used for vacherin type sweets (large rounds of meringue filled with whipped cream, fruit, chestnuts etc.), as a topping for pies, or for meringue shells filled with whipped cream.

Meringue cuite is the firmer type of meringue, used mainly for pâtisserie work. Proportions are 2 oz icing sugar to each egg white (you can be generous with the weight of the sugar). While for meringue suisse it is best to whip your egg whites by hand in a copper bowl (see the notes on making soufflés), to achieve a greater bulk meringue cuite can be made in large quantities with an electric whisk. If you do whisk by hand, it is quicker to put the bowl of egg whites over a pan of hot water, as the heat quickens up the thickening process.

Meringue italienne is rarely used in the home — it is more for professionals and those engaged in elaborate pâtisserie work. It is similar to meringue cuite but a lighter and finer mixture. It is made with lump sugar, which is boiled to a syrup before being poured on to the egg whites. A sugar thermometer is essential.

Meringue italienne

8 oz lump sugar
6-7 tablespoons water
4 egg whites

Sugar thermometer

Method

First prepare sugar syrup by putting sugar and water in pan; dissolve sugar over gentle heat and then cook quickly, without stirring, to 260°F. Meanwhile beat egg whites until stiff and, when sugar syrup is ready, pour it steadily on to egg whites, mixing quickly with a whisk. Continue whisking until all sugar has been absorbed. When cold this meringue is used as a topping and /or filling for cakes, or to replace cream.

Strawberry meringue baskets

For meringue cuite
8 ½ oz icing sugar
4 egg whites
3 drops of vanilla essence

For filling
8 oz small fresh strawberries
2 tablespoons redcurrant jelly (see page 139)

Baking sheet lined with non-stick (siliconised) cooking, or rice, paper

Method

Set oven at 275-300°F or Mark 1-2. Rub icing sugar through a nylon strainer on to a sheet of greaseproof paper; have ready a pan half-full of gently simmering water.

Put the egg whites in a pudding basin, beat until foaming with a rotary or electric beater, then add the icing sugar, 1 tablespoon at a time. When all the icing sugar has been added, flavour with vanilla essence, set the basin on the pan and continue beating until the mixture will hold its shape.

To test this, lift a little of the mixture on the whisk and let it fall. If ready, it will retain its shape as a thick ribbon when it falls in the basin.

Fill the mixture into a nylon forcing bag fitted with an 8-cut vegetable rose nozzle. Shape into 6 baskets, bake for 45 minutes in pre-set oven. Cool.

Beat redcurrant jelly in a basin with a small whisk or fork and rub through a strainer into a pan; heat gently until clear. Hull strawberries and turn very gently in warm redcurrant glaze until coated. Spoon into baskets.

To make a large meringue basket, see overleaf.

Large meringue basket

For a 7-inch diameter basket that will give 6-8 portions, you will need double the quantity of ingredients as in recipe for small strawberry meringue baskets (see page 127). Make it in two batches because you will find one large batch at a time too much to cope with.

Method

Set the oven at 275°F or Mark 1, line 2 baking sheets with non-stick (siliconised) cooking paper.

Make up the first batch of meringue cuite and put half in a forcing bag fitted with, a $\frac{1}{2}$-inch éclair pipe. Use about two-thirds of this to shape one round, 6 inches in diameter, and one hoop of the same size. Bake for 45-40 minutes until dry and crisp. During this baking time keep the basin of remaining meringue mixture covered with a damp cloth to stop it from hardening in the basin.

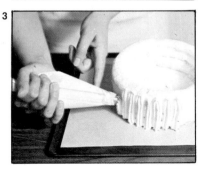

When the round and hoop are ready, turn on to a wire rack to cool and peel off the non-stick paper. Turn this paper over, put back on to the baking sheets and pipe two more hoops of the meringue to the same size as before. Bake and cool as before.

Make up the second batch of meringue and use a little of this uncooked mixture to mount the hoops on the round, one on top of the other. Now put the rest of mixture in a forcing bag fitted with an 8-cut vegetable rose nozzle and cover the plainly-piped hoops with a decorative pattern (see photograph). Bake again at the same temperature for 45-50 minutes until set and crisp.

This meringue case can be made at least a week before a

1 *Draw 6-inch circle on non-stick (siliconised) cooking paper to act as piping guide for a meringue basket. Use $\frac{1}{2}$-inch éclair pipe*
2 *Pipe three hoops of the same diameter (in two batches). When baked and cool, mount on circular base of the basket*
3 *With more meringue mixture, pipe decoration on to hoops; bake again, fill with fresh fruit and cream as shown right*

party and stored in an airtight container. Fill with fresh fruit and cream, or ice-cream, just before serving.

The photograph below shows a large strawberry meringue basket, filled, and decorated with cream and whole strawberries

Meringue Chantilly

For meringue suisse
4 egg whites
8 oz caster sugar (plus extra for
  dredging)
½ pint Chantilly cream
salad oil (for baking sheets)
plain flour (for dredging)

These are meringue shells filled
with vanilla-flavoured whipped
cream. This quantity will make
12-16 shells (6-8 filled
meringues). Unfilled shells may
be stored for up to 2 days in an
airtight container.

Method

Set oven at 250-275°F or
Mark ½-1. Brush 2 baking
sheets lightly with oil and
dredge with flour. Bang sheets
on the table to distribute the
flour evenly, or line the sheets
with non-stick (silicone) kitchen
paper.

Whisk the egg whites until
quite stiff; they should look
smooth and when a little is
lifted on the whisk it should
remain in position when shaken.
For each egg white whisk in 1
teaspoon of sugar for 1 minute
only. Fold in remaining sugar
with a metal spoon.

Put meringue into a forcing
bag with a plain nozzle and pipe
shells on to prepared baking
sheets (or put out in spoonfuls).
Dredge with caster sugar and
leave for a few minutes before
putting into oven to allow the
sugar to melt slightly, giving a

*Taking up meringue mixture with
two spoons to form shell shape*

*Laying shells on to baking sheet
before dredging with caster sugar*

crystallised effect to the meringues when cooked.

Bake for about 1 hour, changing round the trays halfway through (top shelf being warmer than second shelf). When meringues are set, carefully lift them from the sheet with a sharp knife, or peel off the non-stick paper.

Gently press underneath to form a hollow, put back on the sheets on their sides, and replace in the oven to allow the undersides to dry for 20-30 minutes. Lift on to a rack to cool.

The shells are hollowed so that they can hold a fair proportion of cream and the two halves will not slip when sandwiched together.

A meringue of this type should be delicate beige in colour, crisp in texture and slightly sticky.

Serve within 1-2 hours of filling with Chantilly cream.

Alternatively, piping out shells with plain nozzle before baking

Chantilly cream

Turn $\frac{1}{2}$ pint of double cream into a cold basin and, using a fork or open wire whisk, whisk gently until it thickens. Add 3-4 teaspoons caster sugar to taste and 2-3 drops of vanilla essence and continue whisking until the cream will hold its shape.

For a delicate flavour, instead of the essence, sweeten with vanilla sugar (made by storing 1-2 vanilla pods in a jar of sugar), and a few of the seeds scraped from a vanilla pod.

Meringue topping

For meringue suisse
2 egg whites
4 oz caster sugar (plus extra for dredging)

This quantity of meringue suisse will be sufficient for a pudding or pie for 4-6 people.

Method

Set oven at 300°F or Mark 2. Make meringue suisse, as in previous recipe, and pile on to the pudding or pie. Dredge with caster sugar and leave for a few minutes before putting in oven.

Cook for about 30 minutes, until the meringue is a delicate brown and crisp on the top. The inside should have the consistency of a marshmallow — white, firm and easy to cut.

Dacquoise

3 oz almonds
4 egg whites
8 oz caster sugar
pinch of cream of tartar

For filling
4 oz dried apricots (soaked
   overnight in water)
strip of lemon rind
4 oz granulated sugar
$\frac{1}{4}$ pint water
juice of $\frac{1}{2}$ lemon
$\frac{1}{2}$ pint double cream
caster sugar (to taste)

For decoration
2 tablespoons icing sugar (sifted)
1 oz plain block chocolate (grated)
extra double cream

*2 baking sheets lined with non-stick
(siliconised) kitchen paper*

Method
Set the oven at 275°F or Mark 1.
Blanch the almonds, dry well
and pass through a nut mill.
Watchpoint It is important for
this recipe that the almonds are
juicy and freshly ground, so if
you have only ready-blanched
almonds, pour boiling water over
them and leave them to soak for
10 minutes.

Whisk the egg whites until stiff,
add 1 tablespoon of the caster
sugar and the cream of tartar
and continue whisking for 1
minute. Fold in the remaining
caster sugar and the almonds.

Divide the mixture between
the baking sheets and spread
carefully into two rounds, 8
inches in diameter. Bake for
about 1 hour in the pre-set oven.
To test if the dacquoise is done,
lift the corner of the paper and
if it peels away from the bottom

*To test if dacquoise is done, lift
corner of paper ; if it peels away
easily, the mixture is ready*

*Filling dacquoise with cream and
a little apricot purée. Finish with
more cream and grated chocolate*

the mixture is ready (if not, continue baking until this happens). Leave to cool.

Stew the apricots gently in their soaking liquid with a strip of lemon rind to flavour. When tender, rub apricots through a fine sieve and leave to cool.

Whip the cream, sweeten to taste, and mix in a little of the apricot purée to flavour (about a quarter to a third); put into the dacquoise. Dust the top with icing sugar and decorate with rosettes of cream and grated chocolate (see photograph below).

Dissolve the granulated sugar in the water, add the lemon juice and boil for 3 minutes to make a sugar syrup. Dilute the remaining apricot purée with the sugar syrup and serve this sauce separately.

Coffee and walnut galette

4 egg whites
8 oz caster sugar
24 walnut kernels
extra caster, or icing, sugar (for
   dusting)
¾ pint double cream

For filling
1 pint strong black coffee
3 tablespoons custard powder
sugar (to taste)

*2 baking sheets lined with non-stick
(siliconised) cooking paper;
forcing bag and ½-inch plain nozzle*

Method
Set oven at 290°F or Mark 1.

Whip egg whites until stiff but not dry, add 1 tablespoon of the sugar and' continue whisking for about 30 seconds; then, using a metal spoon, cut and fold in the remaining sugar. Put mixture in the forcing bag and pipe out an 8-inch round on one baking sheet; dust lightly with sugar and let it stand while shaping rest of mixture into very small rounds on the second baking sheet.

Place a walnut half on top of each meringue and dust with a little sugar. Put the plain round on a shelf about halfway in the oven and the small meringues on the shelf underneath. Bake until crisp and biscuit-coloured (about 1 hour). Cool meringues on a wire rack.

To prepare filling: make the custard, using black coffee in place of milk, and sweeten to taste. Cover the custard to prevent a skin forming and beat thoroughly from time to time as it cools.

Chop remaining walnuts and whip cream until soft. When the coffee mixture is quite cold, fold in half the cream and the walnuts. Stick the small meringues around the edge of the large round, fixing them in position with a little whipped cream. Fill the centre with coffee filling and decorate this with a lattice of piped cream.

Appendix

Notes and basic recipes

Aspic jelly

This is a jelly made from good fish, chicken, or meat stock very slightly sharpened with wine and a few drops of wine vinegar. Care must be taken that the stock is well flavoured and seasoned and that it is not too sharp, only pleasantly acidulated.

Basic recipe

2½ fl oz sherry
2½ fl oz white wine
2 oz gelatine (see note right)
1¾ pints cold stock (see page 139)
1 teaspoon wine vinegar
2 egg whites

Method

Add wines to gelatine and set aside. Pour cold stock into scalded pan, add vinegar. Whisk egg whites to a froth, add them to the pan, set over moderate heat and whisk backwards and downwards until the stock is hot. Then add gelatine, which by now will have absorbed the wine, and continue whisking steadily until boiling point is reached.

Stop whisking and allow liquid to rise to the top of the pan; turn off heat or draw pan aside and leave to settle for about 5 minutes, then bring it again to the boil, draw pan aside once more and leave liquid to settle. At this point the liquid should look clear; if not, repeat the boiling-up process.

Filter the jelly through a scalded cloth or jelly bag and cool before use.

Béchamel sauce

½ pint milk
1 slice of onion
1 small bayleaf
6 peppercorns
1 blade mace
¾ oz butter
½ oz plain flour
salt and pepper

Method

Put onion and spices in the milk and heat gently, without boiling, in a covered saucepan for 5-7 minutes.

Pour off into a jug and wipe out the pan. Melt the butter in this, and stir in the flour off the heat. Strain in a good third of the milk, blend and add remaining milk. When thoroughly mixed, season lightly, return to the heat and stir continually until boiling. Boil for 2-3 minutes, then adjust the seasoning.

Court bouillon for shellfish

Slice 2 medium-size onions and a carrot, soften them slowly in ½ oz butter, using a pan large enough to hold the shellfish. Add the juice of ½ lemon, a large bouquet garni, 6 peppercorns, 2 pints water, ¼ pint white wine and 1 teaspoon salt. Simmer together for 15-20 minutes.

French dressing

1 tablespoon vinegar (red or white wine, or tarragon)
½ teaspoon salt
½ teaspoon black pepper (ground from mill)
fresh chopped herbs (thyme, marjoram, basil or parsley) — optional
3 tablespoons olive oil, or groundnut oil

True French dressing does not have sugar, but for English tastes add a good pinch. When herbs are added to French dressing it is called **vinaigrette**.

Method

Mix vinegar with the seasonings, add oil and when the dressing thickens, taste for correct seasoning. More salt should be added if the dressing is sharp yet oily. Quantities should be in the ratio of 1 part vinegar to 3 parts oil.

Gelatine

The best is obtained from simmering calves feet in water and is especially delicate in flavour. Most powdered gelatine is obtained from the bones or tissues of animals or fish by boiling. Always use a good quality gelatine and check the amount required with manufacturers' directions.

Horseradish cream

2 tablespoons horseradish (freshly grated)
1 dessertspoon white wine vinegar
1 teaspoon dry mustard
1 rounded teaspoon caster sugar
pinch of salt
black pepper (ground from mill)
1 small carton (2½ fl oz) double cream cream

Method

Mix the vinegar and seasonings together and add the horseradish. Lightly whip the cream and mix gently into the other ingredients.

When fresh horseradish is unobtainable, use grated horseradish preserved in vinegar and mix the seasoning with only 1 teaspoon of vinegar.

Lobster (preparation)

To boil a lobster, rinse it quickly in cold water, have a court bouillon (see opposite), or salted water, ready on the boil. Put in the live lobster, making sure there is sufficient liquid to cover it. Cover pan, reboil and simmer gently, allowing 20 minutes for a lobster 1 lb in weight, 30 minutes for 1½ lb, and over that weight, 45 minutes. Draw pan aside and cool the lobster in the liquid. Lift out and allow lobster to get quite cold. To shell it, split the lobster in two, remove sac and intestine and twist off the big claws. Crack these and carefully lift out the meat, removing the piece of membrane which lies down the middle of the claw. Twist (or snip off with scissors) the small claws, being careful to keep the creamy part in the head. Using the handle of a wooden spoon, roll the small claws to extract the meat. Lift out the tail meat with the point of a small knife.

Mayonnaise

2 egg yolks
salt and pepper
dry mustard
¾ cup salad oil
2 tablespoons wine vinegar

This recipe will make ½ pint of mayonnaise.

Method

Work egg yolks and seasonings with a small whisk or wooden spoon in a bowl until thick; then start adding the oil drop by drop. When 2 tablespoons of oil have been added this mixture will be very thick. Now carefully stir in 1 teaspoon of the vinegar.

The remaining oil can then be added a little more quickly, either 1 tablespoon at a time and beaten thoroughly between each addition until it is absorbed, or in a thin steady stream if you are using an electric beater.

When all the oil has been absorbed, add remaining vinegar to taste, and extra salt and pepper as necessary.

To thin and lighten mayonnaise add a little hot water. For a coating consistency, thin with a little cream or milk.

Eggs should not come straight from the refrigerator. If oil is cloudy or chilled, it can be slightly warmed which will lessen the chances of eggs curdling. Put oil bottle in a pan of hot water for a short time.

Watchpoint Great care must be taken to prevent mayonnaise curdling. Add oil drop by drop at first, and then continue adding it very slowly.

If mayonnaise curdles, start with a fresh yolk in another bowl and work well with seasoning, then add the curdled mixture to it very slowly and carefully. When curdled mixture is completely incorporated, more oil can be added if the mixture is too thin.

Mornay sauce

1 oz butter
2 tablespoons plain flour
½ pint milk
3 tablespoons cheese (grated)

Mornay sauce is basically a béchamel sauce to which cheese has been added. The milk may be flavoured as for béchamel sauce.

Method
Melt the butter gently, take away from heat and stir in flour. Pour on one-third of the milk and blend well before adding the rest.

Season lightly before returning to heat and keep stirring until the mixture boils. Continue boiling for 1-2 minutes, then gradually beat in cheese.

Nuts

To brown hazelnuts (already shelled) : do not blanch first but bake for 7-8 minutes in a moderate oven at 350°F or Mark 4, then rub briskly in a rough cloth to remove skin.

Almonds : buy them with their skins on. This way they retain their oil better. Blanching to remove the skins gives extra juiciness.

To blanch almonds : pour boiling water over the shelled nuts, cover the pan and leave until cool. Then the skins can be easily removed (test one with finger and thumb).

Drain, rinse in cold water, and press skins off with fingers. Rinse nuts, dry thoroughly.

To brown blanched almonds : bake as for hazelnuts (above).

To chop almonds : first blanch, skin, chop and then brown them in the oven, if desired.

To shred almonds : first blanch, skin, split in two and cut each half lengthways in fine pieces. These can then be used as they are or browned quickly in the oven, with or without a sprinkling of caster sugar.

To flake almonds : first blanch, skin, and cut horizontally into flakes with a small sharp knife.

To grind almonds : first blanch, skin, chop and pound into a paste (use a pestle and mortar, or a grinder, or the butt end of a rolling pin). Home-prepared ground almonds taste much better than the ready ground variety.

Poaching fruit

The most important point to remember when cooking fruit is that the water and sugar should first be made into a syrup. An average proportion for this syrup is 3 rounded tablespoons of granulated sugar to ½ pint water per lb of fruit. Heat gently in a pan to dissolve sugar, boil rapidly for 2 minutes before the fruit is added. The syrup may be flavoured with pared lemon rind or a vanilla pod.

Watchpoint Do not add any extra sugar with the fruit even if it is very sour, because too thick a syrup tends to toughen the skins of some fruit while cooking. If the fruit is excessively sour, it is better to add a little extra sugar when the fruit is tender and still hot.

Puff pastry

8 oz plain flour
pinch of salt
8 oz butter
1 teaspoon lemon juice
scant $\frac{1}{4}$ pint water (ice cold)

Method

Sift flour and salt into a bowl. Rub in a piece of butter the size of a walnut. Add lemon juice to water, make a well in centre of flour and pour in about two-thirds of the liquid. Mix with a palette, or round-bladed, knife. When the dough is beginning to form, add remaining water.

Turn out the dough on to a marble slab, a laminated-plastic work top, or a board, dusted with flour. Knead dough for 2-3 minutes, then roll out to a square about $\frac{1}{2}$-$\frac{3}{4}$ inch thick.

Beat butter, if necessary, to make it pliable and place in centre of dough. Fold this up over butter to enclose it completely (sides and ends over centre like a parcel). Wrap in a cloth or piece of grease-proof paper and put in the refrigerator for 10-15 minutes.

Flour slab or work top, put on dough, the join facing upwards, and bring rolling pin down on to dough 3-4 times to flatten it slightly.

Now roll out to a rectangle about $\frac{1}{2}$-$\frac{3}{4}$ inch thick. Fold into three, ends to middle, as accurately as possible, if necessary pulling the ends to keep them rectangular. Seal the edges with your hand or rolling pin and turn pastry half round to bring the edge towards you. Roll out again and fold in three (keep a note of the 'turns' given). Set pastry aside in refrigerator for 15 minutes.

Repeat this process, giving a total of 6 turns with a 15-minute rest after each two turns. Then leave in the refrigerator until wanted.

Redcurrant jelly

It is not possible to give a specific quantity of redcurrants as the recipe is governed by the amount of juice made, which is variable.

Method

Wash the fruit and, without removing from the stems, put in a 7 lb jam jar or stone crock. Cover and stand in deep pan of hot water. Simmer on top of the stove or in the oven at 350°F or Mark 4, mashing the fruit a little from time to time, until all the juice is extracted (about 1 hour).

Then turn fruit into a jelly-bag, or double linen strainer, and allow to drain undisturbed overnight over a basin.

Watchpoint To keep the jelly clear and sparkling, do not try to speed up the draining process by forcing juice through ; this will only make the jelly cloudy.

Now measure juice. Allowing 1 lb lump or preserving sugar to each pint of juice, mix juice and sugar together, dissolving over slow heat. When dissolved, bring to the boil, boil hard for 3-5 minutes and skim with a wooden spoon. Test a little on a saucer : allow jelly to cool, tilt saucer and, if jelly is set, it will wrinkle. Put into jam jars, place small circles of greaseproof paper over jelly, label and cover with jam pot covers. Store in a dry larder until required.

Stock
Chicken

This should ideally be made from the giblets (neck, gizzard, heart and feet, if available), but never the liver which imparts a bitter flavour. This is better kept for making pâté, or sautéd and used as a savoury. Dry fry the giblets with an onion, washed but not peeled, and cut in half. To dry fry, use a thick pan with a lid, with barely enough fat to cover the bottom. Allow the pan to get very hot before putting in the giblets and onion, cook on full heat until lightly coloured. Remove pan from heat before covering with 2 pints of cold water. Add a large pinch of salt, a few peppercorns and a bouquet garni (bayleaf, thyme, parsley) and simmer gently for 1-2 hours. Alternatively, make the stock when you cook the chicken by putting the giblets in the roasting tin around the chicken with the onion and herbs, and use the measured quantity of water. This is preferable to bouillon cube stock for, in reducing the liquid with bouillon, there is the danger of the finished sauce being too salty.

Mixed stock
If you want a really clear stock, the only way to make it is to use raw bones. If you are using cooked ones as well, it helps to add these after the stock has come to the boil, although it is better not to mix raw with cooked bones if the stock is to be kept for any length of time.

Any trimmings or leftovers in the way of meat can go into your regular stockpot : chicken carcasses and giblets (but not the liver) ; bacon rinds ; or a ham or bacon bone. This last is often given away and it makes excellent stock for a pea soup.

Add a plateful of cut-up root vegetables, a bouquet garni, 5-6 peppercorns, and pour in enough cold water to cover the ingredients by two-thirds. Salt very lightly, or not at all if there is a bacon bone in the pot. Bring slowly to the boil, skim, half-cover the pan and simmer 1½ -2 hours or longer, depending on the quantity of stock being made. The liquid should reduce by about a third. Strain off and, when the stock is cold, skim well to remove any fat. Throw away the ingredients unless a fair amount of raw bones have been used, in which case more water can be added and a second boiling made.

If the stock is to be kept several days, or if there is a fair proportion of chicken in it, bring to the boil every day. If you are keeping it in the refrigerator, save room by storing, covered, in a jug instead of a bowl. Remember that the stronger the stock, the better it will keep.

Watchpoint Long slow simmering is essential for any meat stock. It should never be allowed to boil hard as this will result in a thick muddy-looking jelly instead of a semi-clear one.

Sugar syrup
For sugar syrup to keep in store, dissolve 8 oz granulated, or lump, sugar in ¾ pint water over gentle heat. Bring to the boil and boil for 10 minutes.

Tomato sauce
1 oz butter
1 rounded dessertspoon plain flour
½ pint stock, or water
1 lb tomatoes, or 1 small can
  (15 oz) tomatoes
bouquet garni
salt and pepper
pinch of sugar (to season)
1 teaspoon canned, or tube, tomato
  purée (optional)

Method
Melt the butter in a pan, stir in the flour. Draw pan off the heat, blend in the stock or water and stir until boiling.

Cut the tomatoes in half (after wiping them if fresh), and squeeze to remove seeds. Strain seeds to obtain juice only. Place tomatoes and juice into the sauce and add bouquet garni. Season and add-tomato purée to strengthen flavour if necessary. Cover pan and cook gently for 25-35 minutes until tomatoes are pulpy. Remove bouquet garni and turn sauce into a strainer. Press it through, return to the rinsed-out pan, adjust seasoning and boil gently for about 5 minutes or until it is the right consistency.

Watchpoint A tomato sauce must have a flowing consistency as opposed to a coating one. The appearance is improved by stirring in $\frac{1}{2}$ oz butter just before serving. This will give the sauce a good gloss.

Tomatoes (preparation)

To skin tomatoes : place them in a bowl, scald by pouring boiling water over them, count 12, then pour off the hot water and replace it with cold. The skin then comes off easily.

White sauce

$\frac{3}{4}$ **oz butter**
1 rounded tablespoon plain flour
$\frac{1}{2}$ **pint milk**
salt and pepper

A white sauce is quick and easy, made in exactly the same way and with same proportions as béchamel, but the milk is not flavoured. It can be used as the base for cheese, onion or other sauces with pronounced flavour, but béchamel is better for mushroom and egg sauces.

Method
Melt the butter in a small pan, remove from heat and stir in the flour. Blend in half the milk, then stir in the rest. Stir this over moderate heat until boiling, then boil gently for 1-2 minutes. Season to taste.

Glossary

Bain-marie (au) To cook at temperature just below boiling point in a bain-marie (a saucepan standing in a larger pan of simmering water). Used in the preparation of sauces, creams and food liable to spoil if cooked over direct heat. May be carried out in oven or on top of stove. A double saucepan gives similar result. Sauces and other delicate dishes may be kept hot in a bain-marie at less than simmering heats.

Blanch To whiten meats and remove strong tastes from vegetables by bringing to boil from cold water and draining before further cooking. Green vegetables should be put into boiling water and cooked for up to 1 minute.

Bouquet garni A bunch of herbs traditionally made up of 2-3 parsley stalks, a pinch of thyme and a bayleaf, tied with string if used in liquids which are later strained. Otherwise herbs are tied in a piece of muslin for easy removal before serving the dish.

Croûte Small round of bread, lightly toasted or fried, spread or piled up with a savoury mixture, also used as a garnish.

Croûton Small square or dice of fried bread or potato to accompany purée or cream soups.

Dégorger To remove impurities and strong flavours before cooking by : 1. Soaking food, eg. uncooked ham, in cold water for specified length of time. 2. Sprinkling sliced vegetables, eg. cucumber, with salt, covering with heavy plate, leaving up to 1 hour, and pressing out excess liquid with a weighted plate.

Garlic butter A savoury butter made by mixing a clove of crushed garlic to 2 oz softened, unsalted butter. Serve chilled, in pats.

Infuse To steep in liquid (not always boiling) in warm place to draw flavour into the liquid.

Lardons Small $\frac{1}{4}$-inch thick strips of fat about $1\frac{1}{2}$ inches long, cut from piece of larding bacon, which is solid fat. Used to give extra fat to cuts of meat that have little or none of their own, to protect them from drying out during cooking. These strips are larded or sewn into the meat with a larding needle.

Refresh To pour cold water over previously blanched and drained food. This sets vegetable colours, cleans meat and offal.

Roux Fat and flour liaison (mixture). This is the basis of all flour sauces. The weight of fat should generally be slightly more than that of flour.

Sauté To brown food in butter, or oil and butter. Sometimes cooking is completed in a 'small' sauce — ie. one made on the food in the sauté pan.

Scald 1. To plunge into boiling water for easy peeling. 2. To heat a liquid, eg. milk, to just under boiling point.

Tammy strainer Sieve made of very fine double-mesh wire. When a sauce is strained through a tammy strainer, it becomes very smooth and acquires a high gloss as a result of emulsification.

Vanilla sugar Sugar delicately flavoured with vanilla (made by storing 1-2 vanilla pods in a jar of sugar).

Index

143